The Muslim Mind on Trial

Divine Revelation
versus
Secular Rationalism

The Muslim Mind on Trial

Divine Revelation
versus
Secular Rationalism

Abdessalam Yassine

Translated from the Arabic
by Muhtar Holland

Justice and Spirituality Publishing
Iowa City, Iowa, USA • 2003

Printed in the U.S.A.

Published by
Justice and Spirituality Publishing
P.O. Box 2701
Iowa City, IA 52244
U.S.A.

Web site: http://www.JSpublishing.net

ISBN 0-9675795-1-1

Library of Congress Catalog Card Number 20-02101758

Printed on acid-free paper

The interpretation of the Qur'anic verse on the front cover is
And who can baptize better than God? {ومن أحسن من الله صبغة}
(Qur'an 2:138).

Contents

Translator's Foreword

WHEN I FIRST EMBARKED on this translation of Imam Abdessalam Yassine's *The Muslim Mind on Trial,* I was already convinced that the work would be of considerable interest and value to many English-speaking readers, Muslims and non-Muslims alike. That was before the catastrophic events of September 11th, 2001. Since that date, we have witnessed an astronomical increase in what amounts to hunger and thirst for knowledge and understanding of Islam. In the courtroom where the trial of the Muslim mind is being conducted, the public gallery is now jam-packed each day, and the session lasts around the clock. The proceedings are constantly broadcast by the media, so it is hard to turn on the radio or television without finding oneself involved in some aspect of the trial. Muslims from all walks of life are interviewed by reporters, in many countries and in various situations, in mosques and marketplaces, in homes and offices. . . . Panels of Muslim and non-Muslim scholars engage in discussions about Islamic beliefs and practices, the history of Islam and its relations with the West. Members of the public send in their questions and comments, by telephone, fax and e-mail. For authors of books on Islamic subjects, the advertising opportunities are unprecedented.

For obvious reasons, one question arises again and again and again, in private conversations and in public debates: "What is the truly Islamic view of terrorism?"

The reader is sure to wonder how Imam Yassine might answer that burning question. Let me therefore consult the work of a fellow translator, who clearly has close affinity with the Imam. Martin Jenni translated Imam Yassine's *Islamiser la modernité* from French into English, under the title *Winning the Modern World for Islam.*[1] In his Translator's Foreword, he describes the Imam as "the inspired Qur'anic scholar and beloved teacher." In a note to his Foreword, he explains what the author means by the term "Islamist":

> "Islamist" . . . names an observant Muslim, someone whose life source is *islam* in the sense of submission to God. Such persons may well strive for the creation of a society guided by this principle, but it is a grievous (and often intentionally vicious) misuse of the term to represent a religious fanatic or, worse still, terrorist.

In the media programs constantly aired these days, there is at least some recognition of the terrorism inflicted on Muslim peoples, in the form of ethnic cleansing, for instance. Imam Yassine is extremely forthright in his condemnation of such atrocities. In *The Muslim Mind on Trial*, the reader will find numerous passages to that effect, notably the following:

> The modern age is in crisis. Let us not be deluded by what others have built, such as scientific skyscrapers strewn all around. . . . For them, the human being has no meaning except the egoism of the strong, the wasteful consumption of the wealthy, the pleasure of the rich and the death of the poor in the Somalia of starvation and civil war, or in the Bosnia of annihilation, savage slaughter and ethnic cleansing.

Does this mean that Muslims should respond by launching suicidal attacks against the skyscrapers of New York? Not according to Imam Yassine, for he goes on to say:

> The Muslims are closely linked to the world as human beings. . . . We are the envoys of mercy, truth and justice for the world. . . . The choice of the free Muslim mind is that we should strive with all our efforts, so that, some day in the future if God will, we may lead the human caravan, while being fully aware of the content of our Message and duties toward human beings and all other creatures.

Let us now consider the book's subtitle: Divine Revelation *versus* Secular Rationalism. Many readers are likely to be startled by his scathing disparagement of secular rationalism, while many will no doubt be mystified, at the outset, by the sovereignty assigned to Revelation (whatever that may be!). Where the latter is concerned, the chapter entitled *What Is Revelation?* will surely prove invaluable. As for the sources and nuances of secular rationalism and its historical development, a splendidly succinct account of the *"isms"* is provided in the chapter headed *Dumps . . . and Dumps*. However scathing he may be in his description of those "dumps" heaped upon the Muslims, Imam Yassine cannot be accused of exempting them from responsibility for their sick and impoverished condition. In the chapter *Comparison . . . and a Comparison*, he lays that responsibility fairly and squarely on its fundamental cause:

> Our illness is perpetuated and the servitude of our minds is reinforced, because we refuse to acknowledge our own faults. We take pleasure in

criticizing others; we shy away from the duty of stern self-confrontation
. . . [The human being] will not hear from us unless we remedy our faults,
cure ourselves of our diseases and, through self-discipline first of all, gain
virtues and strength.

At this point, I feel obliged to acknowledge my faults in rendering the
author's Arabic text into English. If those faults are fewer and less serious than they would otherwise have been, the credit is due to my Muslim brother in Morocco, Farouk Bouasse, whose editorial feedback has
been invaluable, as well as to my dear wife Nuraisjah, who listened with
amazing patience while I read and re-read my work-in-progress. I must
also express my gratitude to my Muslim brother in Iowa, Imad Ben-
jelloun, who has served as my international courier at every stage, and
to my dear daughter Aisah, whose electronic skills have kept me in touch
with Imad.

May God bless the author, Imam Abdessalam Yassine, and may He
enable the Muslim mind to emerge from its trial with flying colors.

Muhtar Holland

Author's Introduction

CONSIDER THE MIND of one who drinks from the pool of secularity, who sees with artificial lenses and whose intellectual bloodlines are the channels for evolutionary philosophical currents armored with scientific proof. Is there an essential difference between his mind and the mind of other people? Is not the mental constitution one and the same for all human beings, whether they are highly educated or more or less illiterate?

As for Revelation, psychologists and Orientalists have discussed the subject and assigned it to the category of abnormal pathological phenomena. I have not placed psychologists between inverted commas, that being a general reference to the falsehood of *jâhilîya*[2] and that which pretends to have a scientific basis for its incoherent ramblings.

As for those men and women who truly believe, and who surrender to the Will of Almighty God,[3] they have the means of guidance from the errors of the deaf and blind materialistic mind; a mind that collides like a bat with the light of Revelation and goes increasingly astray. True Believers, men and women, have with them the Book of God (Exalted is He), the Creator of the human being, the Constructor of human faculties, and the One who guides whomever He will to a straight path.

This gives rise to the special quality of the believing mind and its essential difference from the mind shared by all human beings. The latter is speculative, autonomous, independent, and profane. It is the materialistic mind; a mind that is preoccupied with worldly affairs and veiled from the realities of the *ghayb*,[4] so long as it does not learn from Revelation and does not perceive the light of Revelation.

The issue is not a mere technicality that distinguishes between the believing mind that receives from God, on the one hand, and the materialistic mind on the other. On the contrary, it is an essential distinction. The matter is not an arrangement in degrees, whereby the materialistic, philosophical mind is ranked above or below the believing mind in wisdom and acumen. It is rather a difference in character.

The scope of the materialistic, scientific mind extends to cogitation and logical consideration of cosmic entities. When it attempts to invade what is beyond its sphere, this mind flounders in the oceans of philosophy, academic propositions and speculations.

That is inevitable, unless this mind is overtaken by a mercy from God that rescues it from errant wanderings; a mercy that takes it back to the threshold of *fitra*,[5] where the illiterate human being, who remains in his natural condition intact and unspoiled by his parents and society, is on an equal footing with the philosopher who returns from his wanderings and dissertations.

The threshold of *fitra* is simply the need of every product for a producer. It is one of the intuitions of the primitive human mind that philosophy wrecks, demolishes and dumps in the heap of suppositions. When the materialistic human mind is afflicted with the malady of blindness to intuitions, it accepts the stupid notion that it is self-made.

The theory of the great philosopher Darwin crystallized, and his dogma was firmly established in his mind when he visited the Galapagos. There he studied a nature that had been isolated from the mainland for millions of years, and had therefore evolved its own pattern of life to keep its fauna and flora alive. It had evolved . . . according to his pretension and blindness.

Over a long period of time, the terrestrial lizard had evolved for itself a spacious pair of lungs, so that it could plunge into the sea and devour marine plants when land plants were in short supply.

Over a very long period of time, the giant turtle, the chieftain of the Galapagos, had evolved a style of life and means of subsistence compatible with the natural environment. The turtle gave its name to the islands. *Galápago* means turtle in Spanish.

What had this cunning creature done with itself? In the course of ages, it had developed a long neck that enabled it to reach the branches of the trees.

Darwin climbed on the back of the turtle, his instructor, and discovered the Theory of Evolution, which he then presented to humanity. He made a thorough study of the continents, their plains and their mountains, their deserts and their fertile regions. He found out that the rule of evolution is common to nature: a nature that is self-fashioned and that evolves for its individuals limbs and organs compatible with the evolving environment.

That applied to the lizards and turtles of the Galapagos, to the desert insects and the ocean fish. That also applied to the ape, which evolved itself gradually until it stood erect and used stone tools. It developed its intellect, enlarged its cranium, increased the weight of its brain, magnified its cleverness, shed the fur from its skin, straightened its nose and refined its character. It expressed itself by grunting after using signs, then spoke a language and eventually several languages, and then enunciated sciences and philosophy.

That is how the philosophizing materialistic mind turns in a vicious circle, when its channels are obstructed, its eyes are blind and its ears are deaf to learning from Revelation.

Metaphor and Reality

In the book entitled *Huqûq al-Insân* [*Human Rights*], we have become familiar with the metaphor of the eye of the mind, its retina, its cornea, its lens and the diseases that afflict it. We have also become familiar with the metaphor of the intellectual bloodlines, their circulation, their channels and their functions that are running in parallel with the functions of the biological bloodlines.

Our intention has been to focus on one of the essential realities that Revelation sets forth clearly and repeatedly, and for which it coins parables, but which readers of the Qur'an pass by and fail to notice.

This reality is that the mind is actually two minds. What we call a mind in ordinary language, referring to the faculty that is common to humankind, is not what is called the mind in the Qur'an. The mind [*aql*], in the Qur'an, is the action of an inner faculty within the human being, called the heart [*qalb*]. The mind is a reception of the realities of Revelation by means of the heart. Comprehension [*fiqh*], in the Qur'an, is a knowledge that arises inside the human being, in his heart. Contemplation [*tafakkur*] is a heart-centered movement that meditates upon the universe in order to demonstrate the existence of God.

As for the ordinary practical mind shared by all humankind, it may be a tool for the heart's aspirations for its Creator. Or it may be a tool for the passion that considers itself divine, for the lower self and its appetites, for philosophy and meditation, for influencing components, or for collecting data and making deductions. The perfect use of the instrumental mind is to serve the heart and its aspirations, with a service that is timely, coherent and firmly connected both here and there: here in the world, where it participates with the whole of humanity in the methods of acquiring the sciences of the visible universe, and there beyond the veils of the Unseen, where true knowledge is attainable only by learning from Revelation.

The subject of the "heart [*qalb*]" is mentioned more than one hundred and thirty times in the Qur'an. In no instance is it used as a term for the fleshy pineal gland. The subject of the "mind [*aql*]" is mentioned fifty times in the Qur'an. In no instance is it used as a term for the common tool. The subject of "comprehension [*fiqh*]" is mentioned twenty times, and the subject of "thought [*fikr*]" eighteen times. In every case, the reference is to the faith-related function of the heart.

The instrumental mind obtains its knowledge of the cosmos by means of the senses and the natural instincts, and then by means of the logic that it develops from the investigation of invariables and inter-related consequences. The perfect mind obtains from Revelation knowledge of the Unseen, and from the common faculties knowledge of the visible realm.

The mind that believes in God and Revelation suffers a loss of sight when it closes the eye of the common faculties, becomes incapable of learning from the cosmos and abandons its tool to neglect and rust. It thereby fails to achieve the mastery of worldly life and sits idly in the company of the impotent slackers. That is a shortcoming and a lack of understanding Revelation. God made the universe subservient to us and commanded us to move about the earth, to dwell in it and to compete and strive with earnest endeavor. That is impossible unless we strive to learn how to use this marvelous instrument called the mind.

The common instrumental mind is afflicted by total blindness that negates the sole real vision: the vision of God and His commandment, the vision of Afterlife and the source of human felicity both here and hereafter.

The believing mind is afflicted by paralysis and impotence in this world, if it closes one of its eyes and turns away from competing in the arena of scientific and industrial endeavor, side by side with the common mind.

When the mind is blind and averse to Revelation, it wanders astray. For it finds no guidance to the unique goal that decides its eternal destiny either in the Garden of Paradise or the Fire of Hell. It finds no guidance to its Otherworldly bliss, even if it holds the means of its material comfort in this world.

"Blindness [*amâ*]" is mentioned thirty-three times in the Qur'an, including three expressions referring to blindness of the senses and thirty expressions referring to blindness of the heart.

As a consequence, the functions and operations of the common faculties of hearing and sight are obscured, restricted and ineffective. The listener thus listens but does not hear, the viewer looks but is not guided aright. That happens when unbelief intervenes between man and the radiant lights of Revelation, when doubt severs his connections with the sources of hearing.

Describing the condition of the unbelievers, God (Almighty and Glorious is He) addresses His Messenger Muhammad (God bless him and give him peace):

And among them are some who listen to you; but can you cause the deaf to hear, even though they do not comprehend? And among them is he who looks toward you; but can you guide the blind, even though they do not see? (Q. 10:42, 43)

Such people hear and see the elements of the universe. Yet they are as the Noble Qur'an describes them:

Deaf, dumb and blind, so they do not understand. (Q. 2:171)

When the mind rejects Revelation, disputes the sovereignty of its Lord, and arrogantly claims to be a divinity, it descends in the balance of truth and eternity to the animal level. Glory be to God, Who disdained that mind to the point where it took pride in being an animal, in being an ape!

God (Exalted is He) describes the deaf, the dumb and the blind who do not comprehend:

We have already created for Hell many of the Jinn and men, having hearts with which they do not understand, and having eyes with which they do not see, and having ears with which they do not hear. Those are like cattle—No, they are worse! Those are the heedless. (Q. 7:179)

Their hearts are merely that pineal gland diseased by the opulence of civilization, the victuals of gluttony, and the life of frenzied and fast-paced concerns that keep the individual constantly enmeshed in the madness of materialism. They do not have the hearts required for comprehending Revelation, the ears for listening to Revelation, nor the eyes for enlightenment through Revelation.

Those are like cattle—No, they are worse! Those are the heedless. (Q. 7:179)

Such are they whom God curses, so that He deafens them and makes their eyes blind. What, do they not ponder the Qur'an? Or are there locks upon their hearts? (Q. 47:23, 24)

They have sealed hearts upon which locks have been fixed. These locks are the product of their stubbornness, their arrogance and their apish stupidity.

May God grant us refuge! May God protect us! May God bestow His Mercy upon us!

From and toward the Mosque

Let us start from the sources, from where the Muslim mind began its journey. The primitive, ignorant Arab mind was separated from its primordial nature by psychological factors and worldly acquisitions. Tribal solidarity, blind imitation of ancestors, love of leadership, amusement and pomp were the most important influences that overlaid the primitive Arab nature.

That mind did not have any great achievement in the sphere of civilization. It did not have skyscrapers and ballistic missiles, for instance, or medical sciences that play hazardous games with the physical organs and the genetic code of the human being.

That primitive mind was not filled with the paradoxes of philosophy, ideology and political doctrines.

That mind was not on the brink of nuclear catastrophe. It was not surrounded by the numerous things and ideas produced by its civilization.

The hindrances in front of Guidance were mostly psychological. The chivalrous virtues of honor, bravery, loyalty, self-sacrifice and responsibility were highly valued. On the other hand, socio-political maladies were prevalent due to intertribal warfare and hostility between neighbors.

Indigence and the paucity of water sources in the desert were in stark contrast with the affluence of the merchants of Mecca, from among whom there emerged a man renowned, throughout his life, for trustworthiness, rectitude and honor.

This man, Muhammad (God bless him and give him peace), was of noble descent, unequaled intelligence and aspiration.

Around the Sacred Mosque in Mecca, in the courtyard of the Holy Ka'ba, God's Messenger (God bless him and give him peace) delivered the Message when Revelation came to him. He himself was overcome with amazement when a figure unknown to him alighted in his presence, addressed him, taught him, recited the Qur'an to him, informed him that he was God's Messenger and commanded him to deliver the Message.

Muhammad (God bless him and give him peace) was alarmed. He came to his wife Khadija (God be pleased with her) wondering what was happening to him. His concern was then resolved and he delivered the Message to his people.

One group heard and believed the Message. The Messenger was gradually joined in his religion by the weak and the ordinary people, men and women, under the persecution of the Quraish, the influential tribe that ruled Mecca.

On the other hand, the influential and powerful elite was deaf, for its members did not hear with their hearts. Such is the state of the mind that is stubborn, arrogant and unbelieving.

God (Glorious is He) describes the unbeliever with a blind and deaf heart:

> He considered [*fakkara*], then plotted—woe unto him, how he plotted! Again, woe unto him, how he plotted! Then he looked. Then he frowned and showed displeasure. Then he turned away in pride. Then he said: "This is nothing but a trumped-up sorcery; this is nothing but the speech of mortal man." (Q. 74:18–25)

The verb *fakkara*[6] occurs eighteen times in the Qur'an. With this single exception, all the other occurrences refer to the consideration of the heart.

Thanks to mercy of Guidance, hearts opened; they genuinely heard, comprehended, responded and believed. They acted righteously; their faith thus increased. They listened to God's verses that bore glad tidings and warnings. Their faith consequently increased, and their certitude and disciple-relationship with Revelation became firmly established.

A Birth . . . and a Birth

The Muslim mind was born, therefore, in the courtyard of the Ka'ba, in the Sacred Mosque. Thus began the history of Islam and the history of the Islamic mind. The Muslim mind was born in the Mosque, while the philosophic mind was born in the public arena—the Agora. The Agora is the Greek name for the public arena in the city center. There Greek democracy, the ancestor of Western democracies, was born. Democracy was born side by side with philosophy, while *shûrâ*[7] [Consultation] was born in the womb of the mind that believes in God and His Messenger.

Revelation introduced the concept of *shûrâ* and the believing mind exercised its judgment in order to put it in practice. I seek God's forgiveness! For God's Messenger (God bless him and give him peace) speaks only on the strength of Revelation! If some of the scholars attributed to him independent judgment, it is simply with a view to cover the peculiarity of the Messenger (God bless him and give him peace), and so that the Muslim mind may be liberated from imitation and may exercise its judgment in implementation.

Roman legalism was born inside the Forum—the Latin term for the public arena. Around the Greek Agora and the Roman Forum were the courts, the markets, the banks and the temples. Convened in the middle of the arena were the public gatherings and public ceremonies that constituted the major display of religion.

Religion was on the periphery together with trade, judicial administration and finance. The central social function was the political function of the public arena.

The Greco-Roman Western mind, the ancestor of the modern mind, was born as the offspring of Greek democratic racialism, according to which human beings were two categories: the free citizen, who enjoys all the rights, and the slaves, who enjoy the sole right of survival so long as they obey their master.

The Greco-Roman Western mind was born on the basis of Roman legalism, which charted the map of the world and allotted the wealth of the world to almighty Rome, the stern, civilized, bloody mistress. It endowed the Roman citizen with tremendous rights at the expense of the rest of the world. That world was ensnared in the fetters of slavery, sometimes rebellious but always suppressed by military legions, powerful and well trained.

From the Mosque in Mecca and from the public arenas in Athens and Rome, two journeys began for the human mind. The two newborn babes had an impact on history whose repercussions we are still facing today. We cannot escape the illusions of politics, modernity, rationality and declarations of human rights, so long as we fail to scrutinize what "human rights" represent for each of those infants.

The Sovereignty of Revelation and the Sovereignty of the Arena

The Muslim mind went out from the Mosque into the arena, while the arena was firmly established in the other mind.

When Christianity came to Rome, Athens and the other regions of the West, it found the place already occupied by the arena and the mentality it engendered. Christianity competed to preside over life, but failed to do so until it made room for Greek artistic civilization, Athenian philosophy and legalistic Roman mentality, adopted them and made of them an instrument and attire.

Revelation, on the other hand, embraced the Muslim human being, shaped his worldly mind and baptized him with the Baptism of God:[8]

> And who can baptize better than God? And it is He whom we worship. (Q. 2:138)

Islam broke the sensory and conceptual idols, step by step, and transferred the human mind from devotion to graven images to allegiance to the One Omnipotent God.

Meanwhile, the newly arrived Church embraced the idols of the Agora and the statues of the Forum. It incorporated into its rituals of worship the artistry of the Greek musical chorus, the pomp of the priest's attire and the arrangement of the altar of his Mass. Pictures, icons and crosses were hung, sculptures were set up and marble pillars were erected.

The rightly guided mind stood at the threshold of *fitra*, asking the innate question about the Creator and the ultimate Destiny. It was informed by Revelation of the Uniqueness of God, of the Garden of Paradise as an outcome for the believers and of Hell as a destination for the arrogant. Revelation described the Garden and the Fire as vividly as if the eye could see them.

The Church had distorted the religion of God's Messenger, the Messiah (Peace be upon him), by propagating Trinitarian polytheism and the doctrine of heaven after death. In the language and teaching of the Church, heaven is something closely resembling the phantoms of the Greek Olympus, in which the gods fly, quarrel and become reconciled, then fight again with one another.

Democracy was born as a racial theory. The Western mind, saturated with Roman legalism and Greek mythology, was born as a materialist idolatry. Christianity failed to purify this mind because it did not escape idolatry, but rather became enmeshed and immersed therein.

When discussing the choice between two minds and two mentalities, we have only two options: Either the sovereignty of Revelation, pure and simple, taken from its source preserved in the Qur'an and the *sunna*[9] of His Messenger. Or the sovereignty of the arena, which occupied the other mind with its materialism, racialism and the vagueness of its goals.

The Islamic source, that is the social, human and cultural environment, interacted undoubtedly with Revelation in mutual influence. Yet the strength of Revelation won over the weakness of the recipient.

On the other hand, Judaic Christianity, arriving in a place already inhabited by philosophical culture, segregationist democracy and authoritarian imperialism, was more influenced by the prevailing environment.

When the Enlightenment's revolutionary philosophy violently ousted the Church from leadership in the wake of the French Revolution, the Church departed from the arena, leaving what is Caesar's to Caesar. In fact, such has been its condition from the start. Caesarism, artistic materialism and sensory idolatry remained the sole ideological and military authority.

What Is Revelation?

God's sempiternal providence drew His servant Muhammad (God bless him and give him peace) toward the time appointed for Revelation. When he reached the fortieth year of his life, he was attracted to seclusion and adoration. He used to spend several nights in a cave on Mount Hira.

On the authority of A'isha, the Messenger's wife (May God be well pleased with her), Bukhari and Muslim report that Revelation took him (the Messenger) by surprise in the cave when the Angel Gabriel (Peace be upon him) came and told him: "Read!" He said (God bless him and give him peace): "I replied: 'I cannot read,' then he took hold of me and hugged me so tightly until I felt exhausted." The Angel repeated the action three times and then said to the Prophet (God bless him and give him peace):

> "Read: In the Name of your Lord Who created, created the human being from a clot of blood. Read: And your Lord is the Most Generous, Who has taught by the Pen, taught the human being what he did not know." (Q. 96:1–5)

A'isha (may God be well pleased with her) said: "God's Messenger (God bless him and give him peace) returned to [his wife] Khadija, his heart trembling, and said: 'Wrap me up! Wrap me up!' He kept saying that until terror departed from him. Then he told Khadija what had happened and said: 'I felt afraid for myself!'

"Khadija said: 'Oh no! Be of good cheer! I swear by God, He will never put you to shame! You are kind to your relatives, you bear every burden, you share your earnings with the deprived, you treat guests with hospitality and you help people deal with the misfortunes of life.'

"Khadija then took him to Waraqa ibn Nawfal ibn Asad ibn Abd al-Uzza ibn Qusayy, her paternal cousin, who had become a Christian before the advent of Islam. He used to transcribe the Hebrew Scripture. He transcribed a great deal from the Gospel into Hebrew, even though he was a very old man who had lost his sight.

"Khadija told him: 'O cousin, hear what your brother's son has to say!' Waraqa asked the Prophet (blessing and peace be upon him): 'O son of my brother, what did you see?' God's Messenger (God bless him and give him peace) told him what he had seen. Waraqa then said: 'That is the Law [*nâmûs*] that God sent down to Moses. If only I were young! If only I may still be alive when your people drive you out!'

"God's Messenger (God bless him and give him peace) asked him: 'Are they really going to drive me out?' He replied: 'O Yes! No man has ever come with the likes of what you have brought, not without being treated as an enemy. If your day arrives and finds me still alive, I shall support you vigorously."

This is how Revelation came down to a man who had no knowledge of the Law [*nâmûs*], which God sends down to whomever He will among His servants. He had no such knowledge; he was terrified by the sight of a strange man who addressed him, admonished him and told him to do something that was unfamiliar to him, since he was illiterate. He was not a philosopher well versed in metaphysics nor was he an intellectual well versed in the history of Prophets.

He was simply a man, with a family and relatives, who was engaged in business just as ordinary people are engaged. He was a simple man until *fitra* awoke in his heart. The sight of his heart was then raised toward the highest horizon, that of the question that appeals for a response. He received the special response that God sends down to the chosen few of His creatures—His Messengers and Prophets (Peace be upon them).

We have stated how Revelation came down. Yet this does not provide an answer to the title of this section, which calls for an explanation of the nature of Revelation.

What is Revelation? Everyone can respond with his own conjecture, inference or linguistic definition. As a psychological analyst, the Orientalist uses all his tools to deduce that the man was truthful in reporting the occurrence but he, like others who suffer from schizophrenia, was addressed by the phantoms of his hallucinations.

For the contemporary who disbelieved and turned away after considering, frowning and showing displeasure:

"This is nothing but a trumped-up sorcery; this is nothing but the speech of mortal man." (Q. 74:24, 25)

Others who were deaf to hearing the call would say he was a madman, a swindler and a liar.

According to the Arab linguist, *wahy* means [revelation in the sense of] rapid intimation.

God (Almighty and Glorious is He) said:

And it was not for any mortal that God should speak to him unless by Revelation or from behind a veil; or He would send a Messenger to reveal what He will by His leave. He is All-High, All-Wise. (Q. 42:51)

Revelation is therefore a form of speech by which God speaks to His chosen servants. It comes either for their personal guidance—in which case it is Prophecy—or because He chooses them (Glory be to Him) to convey His Message to whomever He will among His creatures—in which case it is the Mission of the Messengers (Peace be upon them) assisted by Prophecy.

God (Glory be to Him) delivers Revelation to His Prophets and His Messengers by the Holy Speech, just as He delivered it to Moses (Peace be upon him). Or He sends the Angel Gabriel (Peace be upon him), as the one entrusted with His Revelation, to deliver the Revelation by His leave. To the common folk who respond to His Messengers, God (Glory be to Him) delivers Revelation by means of the Messengers (Peace be upon them), as He said (Exalted is He):

And We revealed to them the doing of good deeds, the performance of the prayer, and the payment of the alms-due. (Q. 21:73)

He also reveals by way of inspiration [*ilhâm*], as He said (Almighty and Glorious is He) about the bees:

And your Lord inspired the bees, saying: "Use the hills for homes, and the trees, and the structures they erect. Then eat of all the fruits, and follow the ways of your Lord, smooth to tread." (Q. 16:68, 69)

He delivers inspiration (Glory be to Him) to the angels, the inhabitants of the heavens, as He said (Almighty and Glorious is He):

And He inspired in each heaven its mandate. (Q. 41:12)

He inspires His mighty command to the angels in particular situations, as when He inspired them on the occasion of [the Battle of] Badr:

When your Lord inspired to the angels: "I am with you. So make those who truly believe stand firm. I will cast fear into the hearts of those who disbelieve, so smite the necks and smite of them each finger." (Q. 8:12)

He delivered an inspiration (Glory be to Him) to the mother of Moses, as an act of providence from Him for her fortunate son:

> And We inspired the mother of Moses, saying: "Suckle him and, when you fear for him, then cast him into the river and do not be afraid, and do not grieve, for We shall bring him back to you, and We shall make him one of the Messengers." (Q. 28:7)

To the fortunate among the believers, God (Glory be to Him) inspires glad tidings in their dreams. For, as God's Messenger (God bless him and give him peace) made it known, Revelation would cease after him and his *umma*[10] would be left with glad tidings, which constitute one out of forty-six parts of Prophecy.

Revelation came to him (God bless him and give him peace) and alarmed him because he was not expecting that momentous event. God (Almighty and Glorious is He) addressed him later:

> You were not hoping that the Book would be inspired in you; but it is a mercy from your Lord. (Q. 28:86)

He also said (Glorious is He):

> You did not know what the Book was, nor what the faith. But We have made it a light whereby We guide whom We will of Our servants. (Q. 42:52)

Revelation came to him (God bless him and give him peace). His Lord spoke to him by means of the noble angel. He commanded him to read since reading is the key to knowledge. He taught him the comprehensive answer to the innate question that importunes sound hearts and to which sick natures are blind, of which they are ignorant and heedless.

> "Read: In the Name of your Lord Who created, created the human being from a clot of blood." (Q. 96:1, 2)

In the first sentence spoken by the Lord of Truth (Glory be to Him) to the Seal of the Prophets and the Crown of His Messengers came the answer that God is the Creator, not the idols, the parents, nature or the cunning turtles on the Galapagos Islands that modify their physical organs to suit the environmental habitat.

The second sentence states that the origin of the creation of the human being is inside the darkness of the belly: a clot of blood, then gradually his body is properly formed and he emerges into external existence as a mystery to himself, unless Divine providence overtakes him and renders him alert.

God's Messenger (God bless him and give him peace) conveyed a message to all responsible creatures, human beings and Jinn. Its first lesson is recognition of the Creator, affirmation of His Oneness and adoration of Him.

The Message came to the earth in order to produce heralds and bearers who would assist the Messenger and strive to support him. The All-High, All-Wise (Glory be to Him) chose an illiterate community, devoid of all learning, equipped with few of the accomplishments of civilization, consisting of separate tribes that demonstrated one of the miracles of the Messenger: that of joining them together and making them, after they had been ignorant, the teachers of the world in a short period of time.

In the pre-Islamic period, the Arabs used to worship idols. Each tribe, clan and family had their favorite idol. The simple folk would fashion their gods from carved wood or piled stone, or from bread that they would eat in time of need. The elite of the tribe would import their idols from *Shâm*[11] and the civilized bordering regions. There the Hellenistic arts had been cultivated in the neighboring Arab towns, since the time of the military campaigns of Alexander the Macedonian.

Revelation, recited to a tribe of illiterates, dazzled them with its eloquence and rhetorical style, for they were the most fluent and most eloquent of the Arabs. Because of its challenging inimitability, which none of them could match, Revelation was the most conspicuous of the miracles. Many other miracles also appeared from the Messenger as a Divine assistance, just as they had appeared from all God's Messengers (God's peace be upon them).

Revelation was conveyed by a man known for his trustworthiness, honesty and nobility. Supernatural miracles like the splitting of the moon were manifest to a tribe of illiterates, close to unspoiled nature, unburdened by the heavy load of civilization that envelops the human being in the filth of materiality, artifacts and graven images, be they made of stone or philosophical speculation.

Nevertheless, some members of that tribe had supremacy over others, for they held privileges, positions of leadership and special advantages.

God's Messenger (God bless him and give him peace) was treated with hostility and combated. But some people heard his appeal and joined him in the splendid renaissance about which we read in the *Sîra*.[12]

Revelation accompanied the Messenger (God bless him and give him peace) in all the stages of his *jihâd*.[13] It accompanied him in such momentous events as the *isrâ*[14] and the *mi'râj*,[15] when his Lord (Glory be to Him) engaged him in intimate conversation. It accompanied him in such decisive campaigns as Badr, Uhud, al-Fath (victorious entrance to Mecca), Hunain and al-Usra.

Revelation accompanied him (God bless him and give him peace), providing him and his *umma* with a detailed account of what God had prescribed for them, what He had made lawful and what He had made unlawful. It delivered glad tidings and issued warnings.

For a period of thirteen years in Mecca, Revelation focused the attention of the True Believers, men and women, on the affirmation of God's Oneness and on the Hereafter. Then, after that, it was mainly concerned with urging the *jihâd* by coining parables about the patience and dedicated striving of the previous Messengers (Peace be upon them), with directing Muslims in stalemated situations, and with the rules of the Sacred Law.

Revelation did not eliminate the ordinary practical mind that manages the affairs of everyday life. On the contrary, it put that mind in charge of the common concerns of humanity. For instance, God's Messenger (God bless him and give him peace) told the *ansâr*,[16] when they sought his opinion about the pollination of date palms: "You are better informed about the affairs of your worldly life!"

Revelation did not restrict the alert, inventive mind that manages and interacts with events, distinguishing the harmful from the beneficial and the sound opinion from the mistaken assessment.

That is why God's Messenger (God bless him and give him peace) used to consult his Companions, seek their advice and mediate in their disputes in matters concerning warfare, travel, settlement and wealth distribution. He and they sought guidance from Revelation, abiding by its text and spirit and exercising their judgment in its application to the extent of their ability, in accordance with the purpose to be fulfilled and in keeping with time and place.

Revelation came down to God's Messenger (God bless him and give him peace) by various means. The Companions bore witness and lived with Revelation and its recipient in daily situations. They became convinced of the truthfulness of the Messenger and their faith consequently increased.

God (Exalted is He) said:

And whenever a Chapter [of the Qur'an] is revealed, there are some of them who say: "Which of you has thus increased in faith?" As for those who truly believe, it has increased them in faith, and they are joyful. But as for those in whose hearts is disease, it only adds wickedness to their wickedness, and they die while they are unbelievers. (Q. 9:124, 125)

God's Messenger (God bless him and give him peace) inspired tremendous awe in the hearts of his Companions (may God be well pleased with them). His humanity formed a link between him and them. He shared with them such human characteristics as food, clothing and residence, happiness and hardship, health and sickness, affluence and poverty. On the other hand, Revelation distinguished him by connection with Holiness.

He was the means of connection (God bless him and give him peace). Such was his exemplary quality, as related by God's saying (Exalted is He):

> Say: "I am only a human being like you. It is revealed to me that your God is One God." (Q. 18:110)

The Messenger's human nature meets with Revelation. He was asked by the Companion al-Harith ibn Hisham: "O Messenger of God, how does Revelation come to you?" God's Messenger (God bless him and give him peace) replied: "It sometimes comes like the clanging of a bell, and that is when it is hardest for me, then it shifts away and I remember what was said. Sometimes, the angel appears to me in the form of a man, then he speaks to me and I remember what he says."

The Companions were sometimes visited by the Trustworthy Gabriel (Peace be upon him) in the form of the Companion Dihya, a man whom they knew. They assumed that he was someone they knew, until the Messenger (God bless him and give him peace) informed them that it was Gabriel, who had come to teach them their religion.

From the change in the Prophet's complexion (God bless him and give him peace), they would know when Revelation was descending upon him. According to Ubada ibn as-Samit (may God be well pleased with him): "When Revelation was sent down to him, God's Prophet used to be troubled and his face would turn pale." According to another account, when Revelation was sent down to him (God bless him and give him peace), "he closed his eyes and his face turned pale."

Revelation was a daily event, a familiar occurrence.

Purification and Teaching

The mission of the Prophet-Messenger is not limited to conveying the Message. Some fools belittle the mighty station of Prophecy and the tremendous mission of the Messenger. They compare the Messenger to the mailman, whose duty is performed once he has delivered the letter to its proper address.

The Messenger has numerous missions, the most important of which is what we read in God's saying (Exalted is He):

> It is He who has sent among the illiterate folk a Messenger from among themselves, to recite to them His Signs and to purify them, and to teach them the Book and Wisdom, although formerly they were in manifest error. (Q. 62:2)

Here we have two qualifications of the Messenger: the first is his being sent from God (Glorious and Exalted is He), and the second is his being from among them, his being a mortal like them, his being an Arab who speaks their language in order to explain to them and his being an illiterate like the common people, who are not distinguished by acquired knowledge like Waraqa ibn Nawfal's reading of Hebrew and writing from the Gospel. If he had been versed in any of the sciences of the People of the Book,[17] they would have suspected him of being a second-hand transmitter. A group of his contemporaries did in fact suspect him, for they said:

> "Only a mortal man teaches him." (Q. 16:103)

He is equally suspected by the current Orientalists and the Westernized fringes of the Islamic community.

Two fundamental qualifications must be fulfilled in order for the Messenger to communicate the Message and influence his disciples through exemplary behavior. He must be a mortal man who receives Revelation, who is supported by miracles and surrounded with God's solicitude, grace and blessing. The Qur'anic verse indicates four basic functions: namely, (1) that he recites to them the Signs of their Lord, (2) that he purifies them, (3) that he teaches them the Book, and (4) that he teaches them wisdom.

Recitation of the Signs is a physical communication performed by speech. It is also a communication in which the evidence of the communicator's truthfulness is attested by the tone of his voice, his humility, the clarity and inimitability of what he recites, his obedience to what is revealed to him, his explanation of what is ambiguous, his detailed exposition of what is concise, and his specific treatment of what is general. All that is Revelation because the Messenger (God bless him and give him peace) does not speak from passion.

Then comes Purification that is, as the Qur'anic commentators explain, "cleansing and growth by the blessing and grace of God (Exalted is He)."

Then comes Teaching that has to do with knowledge, understanding and practice. "He teaches them the Book" means he teaches them the rules of the Sacred Law.

"He teaches them Wisdom" means the detailed modes of practice. Wisdom is "knowledge of everything in existence, the doing of good deeds and attainment of the truth by science and the mind."

The sum of these functions relates to one single attribute, that of the purifying instructor. When asked about cleanliness from filth, the Prophet (God bless him and give him peace) said: "For you I am in the position of a parent who teaches you."[18]

A parent who teaches, a teacher who purifies. The two functions are inseparable: the tenderness of the parent, his love, his eagerness for extending benefit, his loyalty, his trustworthiness and his devotion merge beautifully with his competence, extensive knowledge and patience with the disciples. His condescension was such that he taught them the very particulars of the human being, like cleanliness from filth. Such broad knowledge came to him by Revelation in addition to his human wisdom, chivalry and sagacity.

O Human Being!

The religion is a Law and a Method. As the Companion Abdullah ibn Abbas (may God be well pleased with him and his father) explained: "The Law is conveyed by the Qur'an and the Method[19] [al-Minhâj] is conveyed by the *sunna*." The Law addressed the human being and the Method realized the human model.

The Method is an application that is practical, detailed, organized and gradual. The purifying and teaching of the Prophet-Messenger (God bless him and give him peace) were not aimless or haphazard.

The first thing that Revelation and the Prophet instructed was the affirmation of the Uniqueness of the Creator (Glorious and Exalted is He) and the reality of Resurrection, Recompense or Punishment, Paradise and Hell.

The Noble Qur'an forcefully addressed the illiterates who were responsive to the appeal of the Messenger on this matter. It addressed, and still does, the *fitra* of man as a human being and a creature. The major difference between the first illiterates and all human beings throughout the ages is that the former were virtually not beguiled by the lure civilization. In an age like ours, however the human being has his sensory and intellectual horizons eclipsed by the parasites of progress, philosophy, business and prosperity, and aggravated by the sight of paraded opulence.

The Method is still valid, so long as the missionaries have the requisite qualifications of purifying and teaching, and scrupulously follow his model in the transmission of the Appeal.

Over a period of thirteen years, the Qur'an revealed in Mecca addressed the human being with a strong and serious tone. It told him, among other things:

> O human being, verily you are painfully toiling on towards your Lord, and you shall meet Him. Then he who is given his Record in his right hand, he will surely receive an easy reckoning, and he will return to his people in joy. But he who is given his Record behind his back, he will surely cry for perdition, and he shall enter a Blazing Fire. He once lived among his family joyfully; he surely thought he would never revert. But indeed his Lord was ever Watchful of him. (Q. 84:6–15)

It warned him against the delusion of this world and forgetfulness of his being a creature of God. It thereby opened for him a door to recognize the secret of his existence and destination after death:

> O human being! What has deceived you concerning your Lord, the All-Generous, Who created you, then shaped you, then fashioned you in symmetry? In whatever form He willed, He arranged you. No indeed; but they deny the Doom! And yet over you there are watchers, Noble Recorders, who know whatever you do. Surely the pious will be in bliss, and the wicked will be in a fiery furnace, roasting therein on the Day of Doom, and they will not be absent therefrom. And what will teach you what is the Day of Doom? Again what will teach you what is the Day of Doom? A day when no soul can do anything for another soul; on that day the command belongs to God. (Q. 82:6–19)

It addressed humankind as whole, saying:

> O humankind, be careful to observe your duty to your Lord! The earthquake of the Hour [of Doom] is a tremendous thing indeed. On the day when you behold it, every nursing mother will forget her nursling and every pregnant one will be delivered of her burden, and you will see humankind as drunken, yet they will not be drunken, but the doom of God will be strong. (Q. 22:1, 2)

It warned the human being immersed with his kinsfolk in the frivolities of this world, forgetful of his Afterlife:

> O humankind, God's promise is true, so do not let the life of this world beguile you, and do not let the Beguiler beguile you concerning God. (Q. 35:5)

Such are strong signs that move the human being to wake up from heedlessness, to turn away from the playful, foolish path and from oppressing and fighting his brothers in humanity.

> O humankind, We have created you male and female, and have made you nations and tribes so that you may know one another. Surely the noblest among you in the sight of God is the one who is most truly devout. God is All-Knowing, All-Aware. (Q. 49:13)

Such a Qur'anic verse prescribes for that illiterate and for the human being, in every time and place, the ideal course to follow in order to crown his progress in this life here below with winning God's grace and sight in the Hereafter.

To be male or female, no one chooses his or her gender or knows when, where and how he or she will emerge from nonexistence into existence. "Nations and tribes," "colors, languages and history." The human being has found himself ephemeral and progressing towards a certain Destiny.

He does have freedom of choice, in that he may use the capacities he has been endowed with for doing good work, promoting mutual understanding among peoples and nations and performing what is right and proper. Gratitude for being faithful is expressed by conveying to all tribes and nations the mercy of Islam, and the glad tiding that the human being was not created in vain.

Which Education?[20]

For the person awakened by admonitions, and in the light of his knowledge of what is over there after death, the essential duty is to be brought up in the virtues of faith. He must acquire the strength to pass through this world, its tribulations and illusions. If he is ever hurt, he ought to make sure that his soul is not murdered and his core is not disrupted.

Can the researcher in the Prophet's biography, as related by the Qur'an and reported by those who lived with it, find anything holier and more precious than the Prophetic educational Method?

What is the essence of this purification performed by the purifying instructor (God bless him and give him peace)? How did he "purify" them? How was the cleansing process applied to the Arab illiterates, so that we may apply it to ourselves in our time?

The Prophetic Method of the Qur'an was sent down as a Law by the One Who created the human being, shaped him and set him in order. It was applied with wisdom and in timely fashion by a Prophet endowed with grace and solicitude in all his movements.

The Prophetic Method, purifying and instructive, came from the very same source from which came the body of the human being, his mind and his soul. The Method that purified and instructed the first faithful generation will do the same for all generations to come, on the condition that it remains Qur'anic and Prophetic.

The first step taken by the purifying instructor was to spend the night praying, reciting the Qur'an, remembering his God and seeking his pardon.

The third Sura to be revealed is God's commandment to His Messenger and his Companions to perform the night prayer. It is a mode of worship that transfers from heedlessness to remembrance. You have asked, O impoverished mind, about your significance, but do you really wish to know? You have been told in the first Sura that was revealed:

No indeed; the human being does exceed the proper bounds, in that he regards himself as self-sufficient. (Q. 96:6, 7)

Are you free from your arrogance and your self-sufficiency, and do you wish to return to your Lord! Do you really wish for success and the purity of your soul?

> Successful indeed is he who causes his soul to grow in purity, and a failure indeed is he who stunts its growth. (Q. 91:9, 10)

A failure, indeed, is one who buries his soul beneath the dump of unbelief and disobedience.

The Night of Devotion
and the Day of Business

From here purification begins! From here Islam begins! They begin from radically changing your habitual state. From here transformative repentance equally begins.

The third Sura to be revealed is God's saying (Exalted is He):

> O you wrapped up in your raiment! Perform the prayer by night, but not all night—half of it, or a little less, or a little more; and recite the Qur'an in slow, measured rhythmic tones. (Q. 73:1–4)

The Prophet (God bless him and give him peace) had done the night prayer and so had his Companions for many long years. Devoting the night to supererogatory acts of worship, recitation, supplication and humble entreaty has, ever since, continued to be a necessary entrance to the world of purification.

The True Believer who purifies himself is not someone who devotes both his night and day to prostration. That is a worshipper who flees from this world. His status with his Lord does not concern us, apart from noting that he has turned aside from the striving Qur'anic and Prophetic Method in pursuit of individual virtue.

As we are told in the third Sura to be revealed, the Method is:

> The first part of the night is indeed the time when impressions are strongest and speech most direct. You have by day a lengthy performance of ordinary duties, so remember the Name of your Lord and devote yourself to Him with intense devotion. (Q. 73:6–8)

The True Believer's night is for devotion, while his day is for the lengthy performance of ordinary duties like earning his living, and his Otherworldly needs like *jihâd*. The True Believer's worldly life and his Afterlife concerns are inseparable, except in terms of technicality. All his work is *jihâd*, with night devotion extending into the day of business.

The first part of the night, as the time for prayer, recitation, supplication and remembrance, was prescribed for Muslims before the prescription of the five daily prayers.

The first part of the night is the time when impressions are strongest and most profound in their purification of souls, polishing of the heart mirror and rectification of the soul's distortions.

It was a duty at the beginning of Islam. It is now a customary practice for every earnest penitent.

For True Believers, men and women, there are two times: nighttime and daytime. So long as their nighttime is that of devotees and their daytime is that of those engaged in *jihâd*, their life is totally immersed in purity.

If the human being swims in the flood of his daytime labor, and does not allot space for night prayer in addition to the five daily prayers, the pond of his daytime will probably spill over into his nighttime. It will shower him with fantasies and distractions, and he will then be outside the spheres of *jihâd* and purification altogether.

If someone extends the first part of the night to the whole course of the day, and devotes himself exclusively to worship, it is not for us to erase his name from the list of the successful, even if we were to erase him from the list of those engaged in *jihâd*.

Some people deeply rooted in hypocrisy may ask: "What is the point of all this lengthy talk about Revelation, worship, and night prayer? What has it to do with the mind and the liberation of the mind?"

The present book is not a polemical writing that accompanies you in the course of your methods and procedures, so that you may recognize its methodological efficiency. Its purpose is the establishment and re-minding of the Prophetic Method.

Our subject is a movement, prompted by purification and teaching, from the night of play and the day of unrestrained business activity to an organized schedule. It is a movement from a life that is wantonly wasteful to a life that is truly meaningful.

Ritual Purity

Islamic education embraces the entrant into Islam with the testimony of the truth. With it, he rids himself of the false gods that used to rule his life and the relationships that used to vie for his allegiance. He yields to the Summoner to God, the guide to Him, the envoy, the parent and the teacher. That is the testimony that there is no god but God, and that Muhammad is the Messenger of God.

It is a testimony with the tongue, by which the mind expresses its humble submission to its Creator. It thereby returns from its surmises and questions, for which it has no answer, to the teaching of the Messenger and the Qur'anic recitation of the Messenger.

This marks the beginning of comprehensive purification. Cleansing begins with the removal of filth and excrement. The minor ablution [*wudû*] follows the major ablution [*ghusl*]. Water is applied to the whole body by well-known procedures, in sequence and with a sincere intention.

The major ablution removes major impurity, that is, the contamination that afflicts the soul from the action of the body. Dirt is removed from the soul by the water applied to the whole body. Spiritual contents are linked to the senses; the spiritual content of the Muslim is purified by the purification of his body. By the sincere intention, obedience and the following of the Parent-Teacher [sent by God], these daily actions and abstentions, which used to be a habit, are given a new meaning and a new function.

Cleanliness is part of faith. As reported in the Prophet's saying: "God is Pleasant and He loves pleasantness; He is Clean and He loves cleanliness; He is Noble and He loves nobility; He is Generous and He loves generosity."

Cleanliness does not acquire spiritual value, however, except by the sincere intention and obedience to the Law in its method and sequential performance. By the sincere intention and the scrupulous following of the rules, the major ablution becomes a sanctifying practice bearing a spiritual significance. The minor ablution becomes a light that penetrates the body, from the outer members to the organ related to the heart and the soul.

Upon the entrant into Islam from unbelief, it is incumbent to perform a major ablution that relieves him of what has accumulated from the darkness of unbelief and the licentiousness of conduct. The penitent, returning to his Lord from heedlessness and disobedience, does not know what has accumulated on his soul from the darkness of acts of disobedience. That is most manifest if, during his ignorance, he used to disdain the utmost importance of such training practices as the major and minor ablutions.

Islamic education embraces the Muslim from every dimension, beginning with his body, with the two ritual cleansings, the greater and the lesser. If someone neglects ritual cleansing or omits one of its prerequisites, he has no ritual prayer to his credit. And if he has no ritual prayer, he has no Islam.

For this reason, the concern of the Prophet (God bless him and give him peace) with ritual cleansing was very great indeed. He taught his Companions its elements and methods, for both men and women, with precision and in detail.

In the books of Islamic jurisprudence, for this reason, you find copious chapters devoted to ritual cleansing and its methods, the discussion of purified water, its quantity, its color and flavor, the things that alter its nature and those that annul ritual purity. But in these writings by our righteous predecessors (may God be well pleased with them), the space devoted to the Islamic political system and method of government is not half, nor even a tenth or less, of that given to matters of cleanliness. *Shûrâ* in the life of the *umma* is not less important than ritual cleanliness in the life of the Muslim and the sanctification of his soul.

If we were criticized or unfavorably compared by a politician who does not give any consideration to the rites of Islam, we would throw in his face the objection appropriate to the ignorant. We would tell him that something we call *shûrâ*, when practiced by people who do not cleanse themselves, is a mere game and falsification.

If we were criticized by someone who, with good intention, makes the comparison between the abundance of Islamic literature concerning water, filth and excrement, and the absence of literature concerning justice, *shûrâ* and the system of government, we would kindly show him that Islam's emphasis on the individual is of no less importance than its emphasis on the Islamic nature of government. Each is to be placed in its position of importance. If someone lived in the shade of the most perfect of all systems, in the time of the Prophet (God bless him and give him peace) for instance, yet did not cleanse himself or was not proficient in ritual cleansing, his Islam would be a pretense, a falsehood.

Our objective here is to put our finger on the point where the Islamic nature of the individual and that of the public order intersect. The latter without the former is a building without a foundation. The former without the latter is merely crumbs and scum.

We have marked a pause at this stage, so that the tent of the individual's Islam would not be blown away by political winds. For there may come a day when we have established a political system without Muslims.

By what means can a Muslim remain *muslim*, *mu'min* and *muhsin?* By means of the ritual prayer, which is the pillar of Islam. Without ritual cleanliness, ritual prayer is reduced to mere gymnastics, a sport, if you will, a mockery of Islam.

Infidel materialism has invaded minds, to such an extent that some stupid people believe that the *salât* (ritual prayer) is nothing more than weird exercise, that *siyâm* (the fasting of Ramadan) is some kind of rigorous diet, that *zakât* (the alms-due) is a form of taxation, and so on and so forth.

Absent from Islamic literature are the spiritual meanings of the soul–purification performed by cleansing the members of the body and moving them in the ritual prayer, Pilgrimage and the *umra* (minor pilgrimage), attending the mosque and the other rituals. Their absence was essentially caused by the prevalence of the political obsession that resembles the prevalence of stagnant jurisprudence in previous times.

Had we been criticized or unfavorably compared, in what resembles belittlement of the rituals, from outside the territory of missionary work, the matter would be easy.

I heard one of our venerable scholars, in a videotaped symposium circulating among Muslim activists, poking fun at what he called the "water-closet jurisprudence."

He was discussing the profusion of ritual purity's jurisprudence, compared with the political system's jurisprudence produced by our righteous predecessors (may God forgive us and them). But joking and humorous expression, from a renowned scholar, are likely to have very unfortunate consequences.

Who will make fun of us, we the inhabitants of this era who have neglected the meanings of purification, which is the pillar of the Message of the Envoy (God bless him and give him peace)? We have attached too much importance to political issues and have belittled what God and His Messenger have magnified, and what the Parent-Teacher (God bless him and give him peace) has carefully taught, as noticed in his noble sayings.

Which of us are nearer to his Prophetic Guidance and Method, the jurists of ritual cleanliness, its pious observance and general application, or the adherents of political Islam, who meet in session, after the call to the afternoon prayer, in order to plan for the Islamic Caliphate, until the sunset prayer is announced while they are heedless of their prayer? Making ridicule of Islam, they would allege that the prayer is an act of worship and what they are doing is also an act of worship.

The Ritual Prayer

After ritual cleanliness comes the ritual prayer [*salât*], which is performed at prescribed times. Its performance includes the physical postures of bowing, prostration, standing erect and sitting down, the recitation of Qur'anic verses, and the final testimony [*tashahhud*]. Some of its elements are obligatory and some are customary. It involves the correct positioning of the members of the body, the straightening of the row [of worshippers in congregation], and application of the rules governing the prayer leader [*imâm*] and the worshipper who follows his lead [*ma'mûm*].

The ritual prayer is an act of obedience performed by the body and the mind. The ritual prayer is the servant standing before his Lord, conversing with Him, appealing to Him and humbly submitting to Him. The muezzin's call to prayer is an appeal to salvation. The ritual prayer is a salvation. If someone neglects it or fails to meet any of the conditions of its correct performance, with tranquility and humility, his Islam is imperfect. His deeds will not be sanctioned, even if he strives with all his wealth and strength to establish his alleged Islamic Caliphate.

The same applies to the alms-due [*zakât*], fasting [*siyâm*], and pilgrimage [*hajj*].

[Together with the testimony of faith (*shahâda*)], these are the five pillars of Islam, the pillars of the house of the Muslim's faith. If the house of the faith of all Muslims is not based on the firm foundation consisting of the sincere intention of purification and following of the Prophet's Method, your State, O Muslim, is nothing but a village of ants.

The Flavor of Faith

The Muslim tastes the sweetness of Islam. That taste increases whenever he becomes more consciously devoted to his acts of worship and their perfect performance, attending to them with the utmost attention.

The mind that arrives at the threshold of *fitra,* to inquire about the truth, is not left thirsting by the Lord, the Kind and Compassionate Creator. No indeed, He makes it taste the sweetness of Islam. It is convinced by a proof that is far more decisive than the proof of intellectual logic. Conviction comes to it from the comprehensive transformation that penetrates its soul from the details of worship.

For every act of worship there is an immediate reward. For every honest, intuitive question there is an answer.

The Muslim climbs up the rungs of the ladders of *îmân* and arrives at the stations of *ihsân*. His heart tastes tranquility through the remembrance of God. He tastes the sweetness of faith through his contentment with God, his obedience to Him and his loyalty to the *sunna* of God's Messenger.

The Companion al-Abbas (may God be well pleased with him) heard God's Messenger (God bless him and give him peace) say: "The flavor of faith is tasted by someone who is content with God as a Lord, with Islam as a religion, and with Muhammad as a Messenger."[21]

Listen to the urging of your heart, O Muslim, so you may learn when you have begun to enter the boundaries of *îmân*. The signs of transmission and light are that you taste the flavor of faith because faith is tasted. The taste will give you a satisfaction that is more profound and more comprehensive than the satisfaction you obtain from a thinker with whom you discuss the virtues of Islam.

I seek God's forgiveness! I should have said that theoretical discussion and debate are unproductive and an obstacle to God's path.

They would surely be an obstacle and a diversion, unless they are performed in ways that are best. The best of ways is that you repent, take the ritual bath [*ghusl*], perform the ritual prayer and remember your Lord. Your limbs and organs will then be relaxed from the stiffness of habit; your soul will turn in obedience from stubbornness and arrogance. From the depths of your being comes the credible declaration that the ritual prayer helps to prevent indecency and reprehensible behavior, that faith has a flavor, that God is True, that Prophecy is true, and that the Hereafter is true. Your mind will then be on the path of emancipation from its trial that came from its rejection of Revelation, or its disdain for the comprehensive remedy. Similarly, well-being, salvation and freedom will come from faith, belief and work.

Tell me! What is the subject of our discussion? Is it the trial of the mind, or cleanliness and the ritual prayer? By the way, what is the mind? What is the human being? Is it the body? Is it this absent-yet-present, known-yet-unknown entity whom you call "I" though you have no idea what "I" may be?

If the "I" is the mind, if this mind regards the body as separate from the soul, believes its sensory perception and does not believe Revelation, its trial will never end.

The Protective Embrace of Islam

The educational Prophetic Method is a method of *fitra,* not an ideological method. It is a method of practice, not a method of argument.

You enter into the mosque, crowding in line with Muslims. You wait for the time of the ritual prayer, maintaining the state of cleanliness. After a while, your heart is relieved to hear the call to prayer; the spirituality of the mosque enters into you.

> God guides to His Light whomever He will. (Q. 24:35)

Islam enfolds the Muslim in the embrace of acts of worship. His body is the first to be taken care of.

The Law commands him to protect his physical limbs and organs. He must guard the tongue against backbiting, slander, indecency and telling lies. The tongue must learn to say good things when speech is obligatory. It must also learn to keep silent when silence is wise. At another stage, it must learn to enjoin what is right and proper and to denounce what is wrong and improper, once its owner has set himself as a model.

The Law commands him to keep his ear from hearing slander and to shun tittle-tattle foolishness. The Law commands him to lower his gaze at the sight of indecent things, and to enjoy gazing at the text [of the Qur'an] and reciting God's signs. O ear and eye! Is there any way to keep you both safe in this era of satellites and cable television, and their sounds and images of indecency posing as art?

The Muslim must keep his stomach, genitals, hands and feet within the limits of what is lawfully permissible. He must keep his heart safe from holding a bad opinion of God and humankind. He must preserve his private parts with decent clothing. The man has his decent clothes and the woman has her *hijâb*.[22]

Those who oppose the woman's *hijâb* know nothing of Islam. They are similar to those who wish to impose the *hijâb* on the woman as a compulsory garment.

In the context of the Prophetic tradition concerning repentance and education, the discipline prescribed for the Muslim by the Law, and the tasting of the sweetness of faith, the Muslim woman is offered the choice between an appearance that is false, decorative and devilish, and the reality of the body that is honored in the sight of God, if it obeys Him in wearing decent clothes, just as it obeys Him in cleanliness and the ritual prayer.

What does a body that views itself as an animal have to do with decent clothing and *hijâb?*

In the context of public order, public morals and public authority, the Muslim woman's *hijâb* is one of the rites of Islam. On the day when Islamic values prevail, the eccentric will be ashamed of her nakedness and her brazen display of her charms. If she is not ashamed, she will be put to shame.

The Muslim safeguards his body in whole and in part, both its visible and invisible members. He is also careful about what enters his body by way of nourishment. He does not eat pork, carrion meat and other forbidden foods, nor drink alcoholic beverages. He does not indulge in narcotics and bad things like tobacco.

All of these constitute the basic prerequisites for the sanctification of the human being, and the basic rights on which is founded his supreme right—that of knowing God.

A bad soul dwells in a bad body. None will enter the Garden of Paradise except those good men and women to whom the angels will say at its gates:

"Well you have fared, so enter in, to dwell therein forever." (Q. 39:73)

The flesh that grows from forbidden food is most worthy of the Fire of Hell. The members of the body that have neither bowed down nor prostrated themselves before God are the fuel of Hell, unless God pardons them. The body that carelessly strays outside the boundaries of the Law is the firewood of Hell, unless God grants it forgiveness.

The Prophet, who was the Messenger, the Teacher, the Parent (God bless him and give him peace), taught his Companions by setting a good example. Companionship in the Prophetic Method is the necessary entrance to education and purification. The fellowship of the people of the mosque is a fundamental, and so is the fellowship of True Believers. You must sit with them for a while to remember God. Like them you will believe and your faith will increase. That is the protective embrace of Islam.

The Medicine of Revelation and the Healing Power of Prophecy

I n the beginning was God's gracious favor and noble generosity towards His creatures. God (Glory be to Him and Exalted is He) created the human being and shaped him, proportioned him and apportioned for him, then guided him:

> O human being! What has deceived you concerning your Lord, the All-Generous, Who created you, then shaped you, then fashioned you in symmetry? In whatever form He willed, He arranged you. (Q. 82:6–8)

By His gracious favor, His giving, His creating, His shaping and His assignment of the form, in the time and the circumstances, He causes your emergence, O human being, from the realm of nonexistence into the world of existence. Then He will let you live and make you die, bring you forth from the grave and resurrect you, call you to account and recompense you. He may pardon and forgive, since He is the All-Forgiving, the All-Compassionate, or He may punish, since He is Stern in punishment.

You, O human being, are obliged to work and are responsible for your acts, even though God created your work.

This is a first contradiction in the view of the defective mind, a trial and a hardship.

The Muslim mind is affected by the malady of double vision, when the perception of the logical mental sight does not coincide with the faith-related insight of the heart. The result is constant reeling from right to left between the two creeds, namely fatalism and free will, which have incessantly preoccupied the Muslim mind.

The deviant and defective mind, which has not accepted the tranquility of faith, inquires about the mutual existence and arrangement of two mental contradictions in one place.

The open-eyed believing mind accepts what Revelation has brought and what the mental view has deduced. Whenever something is obscure to its logical thinking, it entrusts it in all contentment to the reality that is manifest to its heart: that God is All-Knowing and All-Wise. It sees no contradiction in the simultaneous assignment of action to the responsible servant and creation to the All-Powerful Lord.

People have not ceased to argue about fatalism and the indifference and apathy it brought about for Muslims. It is a frustrating creed, for what is the point of making effort, if everything has been sempiternally predestined? That is a one-eyed question!

The intellectuals among us, disciples of orientalism, adopt the free-will doctrine of the Mu'tazilites, who deny what God prescribed in His Book—that He created us and created our works. That is a most deviant creed!

Let us now embark upon our subject concerning the Medicine of Revelation and the Healing Power of Prophecy. We advise those who complain about double-sightedness to see the Physician and use the medication of the Parent-Teacher (God bless him and give him peace). Guidance is from God (Glory be to Him), Who opens the heart of whomever He will of His servants to Islam, and imbues him with the light of faith and certainty. He (Glorious and Exalted is He) said:

> Whoever it is God's Will to guide, He expands his breast to Islam, and whoever it is His will to send astray, He makes his breast tight and narrow as if he were engaged in sheer ascent. Thus God lays ignominy on those who do not believe. (Q. 6:125)

The servant is notified, at the same time, that he must change his condition:

> God does not change what is in a people, until they change what is in themselves. (Q. 13:11)

There is no contradiction in the sight of one who has two eyes. The relevant practical question is: "How shall I change what is in myself and repent, so that God will relent toward me?" The question may be posed in reverse: "How will God relent toward me, so that I may repent, laying myself bare to His giving by approaching Him (through good deeds)?"

The question relates to the knowledge of how God opens hearts to Islam, and how the Muslim tastes the sweetness of faith. As we have mentioned, the Prophet (God bless him and give him peace) declared that the flavor of faith is tasted by someone who is content with God as a Lord, with Islam as a religion, and with Muhammad (God bless him and give him peace) as a Messenger.

Contentment is a psychological, heart-centered condition. It is a heart-centered feeling and a satisfaction that embraces the human being altogether: his emotion, his mind and the movement of his limbs and organs.

Inform me, O Physician! How are contentment and tranquility achieved?

Is it a matter of clinical treatment, as physicians say?

Revelation responds through the Spokesman, the Parent, the Purifier, the Teacher (God bless him and give him peace). As reported by al-Bukhari and Muslim on the authority of Anas (God be pleased with him): "If someone has the following three virtues, he will discover the flavor of faith: (1) If he loves God and His Messenger and they are dearer to him than anyone else. (2) If he loves a servant for the sake of God. (3) If he would hate to return to unbelief, after God has delivered him, just as he would hate to be thrown into the Fire of Hell."

Those who lived with the Parent-Messenger (God bless him and give him peace) entered into the love of God by the love of His Messenger—a Messenger who is kind to the True Believers, compassionate, gentle and responsive—and they discovered the flavor of faith. After him, every generation has this threefold means of access: anyone searching for *fitra* has to love a servant only for God's sake, and mingle in the mosque with the True Believers whom he loves for God's sake.

This love becomes gradually manifest in the newcomer to the mosque who is thirsty for faith. The companionship of the people of the mosque and the example of the righteous people of the mosque convey him, on the wing of his truthfulness and the sincere intention of his approach to God, to the place where the flavor of faith is tasted.

With them, he performs the ritual prayer five times in the course of the day. He sits in their company and engages with them in mutual assistance. Love for God's sake results in comprehensive satisfaction that is shared by the open mind, the feelings and the aspirations. The mind is thus not captured by arid logic and egoism.

That is a prerequisite. It is a total approach and immersion, not an intellectual curiosity.

The inquisitive, open and truthful newcomer thus obtains an increase of faith, by adopting the Physician's diet and taking the recommended healing medication.

In the Noble Qur'an and in the Prophetic Tradition, there are tens of mercies, tens of stipulated recompenses: "If someone acts thus, he is entitled to such-and-such."

The tasting of the flavor of faith is an immediate recompense, so the seeker is reassured in his journey and moves forward. The tasting of faith and the soul's *tranquillity* in the remembrance of God, however precious, are merely a prelude and a proof of the lofty Otherworldly aspiration.

The aspiration of one who comes to the threshold of the Prophetic medication becomes loftier stage by stage. He begs God for one good thing after another; then his trust in the Noble, the Generous (Glory be to Him) becomes magnified, when he begs Him for the best of this world and the Hereafter.

In the nursing of Prophecy, if someone acts like that until supplication and genuine trust prevail upon him, he will be granted gifts after gifts.

According to a Saying reported by at-Tirmidhi, God's Messenger (God bless him and give him peace) once said: "If someone goes to his bed in a state of cleanliness, remembering God until sleep overtakes him, God will grant him all that he wants, whenever he wakes up for a moment at night and asks God to grant him the best of this world and the Hereafter."

Then the aspiration of the truthful soars, when he becomes prepared for earnest endeavor and *jihâd*. After the well-being felt in the flavor of faith, and the health achieved by asking God for the best of this world and the Hereafter, he begs God for the virtue of entering into the protective embrace of comprehensive care and solicitude.

The stipulations are presented to him by the Prophet-Interpreter (God bless him and give him peace), who said, as reported by Muslim on the authority of Abu Dharr: "God (Glorious and Exalted is He) says: 'If someone brings one good deed (on the Day of the Last Judgment), he shall be recompensed for ten like it, or I shall add more. If someone brings one bad deed, he shall be sanctioned for one, or I shall forgive. If someone draws near to Me by an inch, I shall draw near to him by a yard. If someone draws near to Me by a yard, I shall draw near to him by a fathom. If someone comes toward Me walking, I shall go toward him at high speed. If someone meets Me with a mistake the size of the earth, but without associating anyone with Me, I shall meet him with the like of it as forgiveness."

What a Compassionate God! What a Merciful God!

Some would believe a specialist physician and rely on a particular medicine: a yellow tablet, a red one four hours later and another in the evening. They would yield to the physician once they had felt the agony of the disease in their body and suffered from the pains of the kidney and the heart. No one is so confident, however, that there is a medicine for the hearts and a cure for what is in the breasts, except those who have despaired of their drowsy thinking, their futile action in this life and their wretched bestiality—those who manage to listen for one day, for one hour, or for just one moment, to the appeal: "Come to salvation! [*hayya alal-falâh*]."

The medical method, as described by the Qur'an and the *sunna*, is the following: "If someone acts thus, he shall be entitled to such-and-such." You must change what is in yourself, so that God may change what is in you. You must draw near to Him by means of what He has decreed for you: cleanliness, ritual prayer, the alms-due, fasting, pilgrimage, remembrance of God and righteous works.

As you draw nearer, inch by inch, the Master will double the recompense and shorten the distances.

And you, O ego-mind, will be on the path of emancipation from your trial!

A Globe and an Orbit

The human being is so presumptuous, however, that he sees himself as self-sufficient. According to his conviction, his mind has fashioned itself through its struggle with nature, which he eventually subdued. Will he ever realize that his effort in this life is an idle sport, so long as he does not set himself a loftier goal than pleasure, enjoyment, sex, self-interest and egoism?

How can he realize that his contentment with being an animal is a most serious misfortune, and that his trouble with meaningless toil is like no other trouble?

Once he has rationalized nature, he goes on to rationalize his own soul. He amputates the most important part of his essence, or rather the whole of it. He ignores the dignity of the human being, his sublime right to know God and prepare for the eternal bliss in a Garden as wide as the heavens and the earth, prepared for the truly devout.

The self-centered, grappling, malignant mind is dragged down by its passion into an empty orbit. The Muslim mind revolves around the sun of Revelation, exposing itself to its light and healing rays. The malignant mind disbelieves in every religion, once it learns about the "mysteries" and scandals of the Church.

How quickly the earliest mind of Muslims turned away from the primitive idolatry that used to fashion gods from bread, which would be eaten in time of need!

As for the mind of secular "Enlightenment," it observed how the Church would fashion its god each morning and evening, then eat it, while suppressing anyone inquiring about "mysteries" unintelligible to the "unsanctified" mind.

As he still does, the priest would fashion his deity when the need arose, and feed him to the people. This strange practice is called the "Eucharist." The priest takes a special piece of bread and some wine, which he then "sanctifies." The bread then becomes the flesh of the deity and the wine his blood. He then feeds his Lord to whomever he will.

How could the inventive mind fail to laugh at these deplorable childish antics? How could the inventive, philosophical mind fail to inquire about an orbit on which it could be centered, as a substitute for its subordination to a superstitious Church?

At the head of the Church was the Borgia[23] family. The name stinks in history with the aroma of infamy that cannot be described in writing.

Into the bonfires of the Church, the "Holy Office" would throw human fuel every day in the course of six centuries.

Copernicus rebelled against the Church's doctrine concerning the globe, and proved that the earth revolves around the sun. In the same way, the Enlightenment philosophy emerged from philosophical Copernicism, when Kant changed the established concepts. For him, the mind is the center of existence around which everything revolves.

Schopenhauer placed the will in the center of everything. To put it in our own language: "It is the passion that worships a mental idol, instead of the Church's idols."

The philosopher Nietzsche assigned priority to passion over the love of knowledge. According to him, will power is the sole substitute for the "ethics of the slaves," which have been established through centuries of the Church's intellectual, repressive and opportunistic despotism. A wrestler was he, the crazy philosopher who cast his shadow over rebellious thinking. He epitomized the struggle for survival between life and death, and the quest for "Superman" as the ideal human aspiration.

The mind that embraced Revelation in the lifetime of the Messenger (God bless him and give him peace) was a primitive mind, still unspoiled by the accomplishments of civilization. Thus it revolved around the globe of Revelation in a state of well-being. Healthy and sound, it beamed perfection on humanity for a period of time.

Today, the inherited Muslim mind still clings to its Islam. Yet it is confronted with the other mind, which took control of those minds that are ground in the mill of international culture, just as the malignant devil takes control of a person whom it renders insane.

The rebellious mind is now awake, strengthened by the might of inventions. Will the medicine of Revelation and the remedial treatment of Prophecy be effective in curing it from its contaminating insanity?

Islam: Religion of Community

From the steps of the penitent returning to his Lord, and asking about the meaning of his existence, begins the victorious journey that is protected by the Sempiternal Divine Providence.

These steps are assisted and guided by the light of worship and assurance of the Lord of Truth (Glory be to Him). They are also supported by the medicinal action resulting from the practice of the commandments and the avoidance of what is forbidden.

> The ritual prayer helps to prevent indecency and reprehensible behavior. (Q. 29:45)

Every act of obedience enlightens the mind. Some acts of obedience give the taste of the flavor of faith. Among the principles of medical practice and education comes affiliation with the congregation in the mosque.

The Muslim restrains his own soul, rebukes it, calls it to account and enjoins it to practice truthfulness and *jihâd*. His ritual prayer and pious devotion help to restrain him. His fellow Muslims help to restrain him, through exhorting to what is right and proper and condemning what is wrong and improper. He also cooperates with Muslims in pious devotion.

> But as for him who feared to stand before his Lord, and forbade the soul to follow passion, surely the Garden [of Paradise] will be his final place of rest. (Q. 79:40, 41)
> And help one another to practice piety and true devotion, and do not help one another to practice sin and enmity. (Q. 5:2)

> And the believers, men and women, are protecting friends for one another. They enjoin what is right and proper and they forbid what is wrong and improper, and they establish the ritual prayer and pay the alms-due, and they obey God and His Messenger. As for those, God will have mercy on them. God is Almighty, All-Wise." (Q. 9:71)

The True Believer treats himself as an object for improvement and correction, so as to avoid meeting God with a faulty, deformed spiritual character. He forbids his soul to follow passion and commands it to practice true devotion. Within the community, he uses the currency in circulation: love, truthfulness and knowledge in addition to other virtues of faith and its affluents. He calls himself to account with severity, because he deceives none but himself if he flatters himself. On the other hand, they treat him kindly for the sake of loving affection, but they also advise him, to the extent he can bear, until he grows self-accountable. Kindness toward others is a Prophetic wisdom and custom.

> It was by the mercy of God that you were lenient with them, for if you had been harsh and hard of heart, they would have scattered from all around you. So pardon them and ask forgiveness for them, and consult with them about the conduct of affairs. Then, when you are resolved, put your trust in God. God loves those who put their trust in Him. (Q. 3:159)

The True Believer who joins the community of True Believers strives for the improvement of his soul through self-discipline, as soon as he is convinced that his salvation in the Hereafter depends on his coming before his Lord with a sound heart. His concern, from then on, is to purify himself inwardly just as he purifies himself outwardly.

He purifies himself and draws nearer to God, inch by inch and yard by yard. The mutual duty incumbent upon the True Believers, men and women, is to assist one another in severing the ties with the past of heedlessness and in shortening the distances.

Stations and a Race

I have used the expression "shortening the distances" metaphorically. In fact, there are no inches and yards between God (Almighty and Glorious is He) and His servants. It is simply a way of teaching the True Believers, men and women, that there is a journey and progress to be made. The intention is also to suggest that the matter is a race between the diligent and the lazy, and a competition between someone who takes the journey seriously and someone who dawdles along. Indeed, competition is urged by God (Exalted is He):

> So vie one with another in good works. (Q. 5:48)

> So in that let the competitors compete. (Q. 83:26)

The Muslim who is sluggish, isolated or ignorant does not conceive of the religion as stations: *islam*, then *imân* and then *ihsân*. Lacking incentive, he is not prepared for serious commitment to improve his soul and compete in good works, so that he may attain a station closer to God.

God (Glory be to Him) extols those among His servants who experience a need for God that is pressing, genuine, active, and eager to draw near and to compete. A servant like that will appeal, implore and seek the means of access to his Lord. His whole aspiration has been concentrated and the focus of his heart has been unified. God (Glory be to Him) said:

> Those whom they call upon seek the way of approach to their Lord. Which of them shall be the nearest? They hope for His mercy and they fear His wrath. (Q. 17:57)

The mind and the whole self of that servant are on their way to well-being and release from trial and tribulation.

Such are unequaled virtues of mutual assistance within the community of the True Believers.

The Dangers of Disengagement

There are corresponding dangers to be avoided. One of the dangers is that the newcomer and his hosts may concentrate on the improvement of their own souls, the enjoyment of the warmth of love, the air of serenity and the intimacy of companionship. In so doing, they become disengaged from the missionary function, shrink together and retire into a closed circle.

That is a deficiency in understanding, a defect in the mind and a paralysis in action. Outside the educational nursery are the scorching heat of the society of hatred, the abominable words and deeds, and the frowning gaze of the sons and daughters of this world. The newcomer and his hosts may therefore recoil from overcoming obstacles, gloomy and intractable, and resort to a comforting haven.

In their isolation, they may feed for a time on the attribution of purity to the self, which is disapproved and forbidden in God's saying (Exalted is He):

> So do not attribute purity to yourselves. He is Best Aware of him who practices true devotion. (Q. 53:32)

The attribution of purity that is disapproved, forbidden and blameworthy is the conceited pride of the worker in his work, the worshipper in his ritual prayer and the bearded man in his beard.

Those who attribute purity to themselves feed by their self-importance on a melancholic time. Their self-importance distorts their vision, to such an extent that they see all other people doomed to perdition, while they will be saved, that all are astray while they are rightly guided, that all are unbelievers while they are believers. They emerge, after that, as an affliction on mankind and the environment.

Which of the two groups is farthest from the Prophetic Guidance and the educational Method: the self-absorbed or the aggressive?

The Training of Missionaries

R ight conduct and the Prophetic Guidance demand that the sojourn in the bosom of education should be a formative stage for training the missionaries in warmth and receptivity, genuine kindness, refinement of speech, and conveying glad tidings to society as a whole.

The function of the small, educational, organized group is to spread its guidance in society as a whole, by striving to ensure that its meetings are appreciated, that people rush to attend its mosque, and that its leadership is accepted.

If the small group withdraws into seclusion, goes on the offensive, or issues charges of unbelief, it will cut itself off from the body of the *umma* by an abominable and blameworthy attribution of purity to itself. It will turn sterile and condemn itself to perdition. Those who retire and isolate themselves may be nearer to safety.

Outside the educational nursery is the scorching heat of a society of hatred, and the danger of melting in an environment flooded with the clamor of life, the ideas of the *jâhiliya* and the obstacles of deviations. Entering into the turmoil of the clamor, conflicting ideas and furious upheavals, is part of the training of those engaged in *jihâd*. It is one of the obstacles on their path, and a test to demonstrate the extent of their patience to assume responsibility for the welfare of the *umma*.

God (Exalted is He) said:

> And We have appointed some of you a test for others: Will you endure with patience? And your Lord is All-Seeing. (Q. 25:20)

In the noble Prophetic Tradition, we are told that someone who mixes with people, and patiently endures their abuse, is better than someone who does not.

Once they have acquired the courage to commit themselves to self-discipline, there awaits the True Believers, men and women, the duty of confronting the other mentality that disregards faith and virtue.

The Profession of Nursing the Sick

Yesterday on the radio, I heard a program involving specialist professors. The title of the program was "Religious Magic." For them, the title is not meant to vilify religion because it contains a form of magic, nor to belittle magic for not being secular. The professors are a class of polymaths, fluent in a number of languages. They have direct connections with the greatest and most famous institutes of research. Being open-minded, they converse with sympathy and tolerance that is paternal, thoughtful, understanding, respectful of all points of view.

Islam and Satan are both satellites in the orbit of the international cultural mind—the supreme judge. Holy Islam and holy Satan are both entertained in its court.

Here, the intellectual who obtains his intellectual provision from secondhand sources, propounds a rigidly inflexible point of view. The intellectual who owes his international formation to paternal sympathy and indulgence is, by contrast, easy-going, respectful of peculiarities and tolerant of contradictions. While the former, from his right-wing liberal or left-wing revolutionary trench, wages war on religion and its legendary convictions, the latter opens his arms to all "sacred things."

The one wages war on his fantasies, just as Don Quixote used to wage war on windmills. The other is securely seated on a radiant orbit, prepared to give every fantasy, reality and peculiarity its cozy place in the parameter of relativity and comparative studies.

But whereas the Don had, beyond his simplemindedness, a goodly nature and great heart, the others are secondhand idiots whose hearts have been imbued with loathing for all sacred things, be they genuinely divine or pertaining to false religion, magic, sorcery and devilry—all of that, for them, is filth and garbage.

The professors talk about the holy devil—which they call a spirit—who is present at the backgammon parties that we call *"dardaba"* in Morocco. They make comparison between the holy local devilry and its likes in China and Brazil. Their arguments about it are well documented and related to their ethnographic origins, African sources, venerable cults, holy sacrifices and music concerts. They are substantiated by evidence attesting to its curing power.

How ought the True Believers, men and women, to emerge from the mosque and their sessions of faith, into a society swarming with superstition, the sanctifiers of superstition and the missionaries of adultery in public?

Some would enter the mosque like the proverbial whirlwind, accusing this person of heresy, invalidating another's ritual prayer and causing trouble and distress. On the other hand, you would find some silent and withdrawn. What wise approach should be used, therefore, in order to address people of all stripes, without adopting a tone that is conciliatory, condescending and defeatist, or one that is hostile and fuming with grief and impotence?

Perhaps among these intellectuals there are great and alert hearts that are prepared to hear the truth, if it comes from the mouth of wise men and women.

The Commerce of This World and the Hereafter

The cultivator of his Afterlife goes to sleep in a state of cleanliness. When tossing and turning in his bed, he asks God for the best of this world and the Hereafter. He performs such righteous works as are stipulated in the commerce of: "If someone acts thus, he is entitled to such-and such."

Whenever Abdullah ibn Ja'far did someone a favor or fulfilled a duty, he used to tell him: "Welcome to someone who carries our provision for the journey to the Hereafter!"

A servant does not draw near to the Loving God (Glory be to Him) except by means of what is prescribed in His Book and the *sunna* of His Messenger (God bless him and give him peace). God (Glory be to Him) has permitted His servants to endeavor earnestly in the commerce of the Hereafter:

> O you who truly believe, shall I show you a commerce that will save you from a painful doom? You must believe in God and His Messenger, and strive for God's cause with your wealth and your own selves. That is better for you, if you did but know. He will forgive you your sins and cause you to enter Gardens beneath which rivers flow, and pleasant dwellings in Gardens of Eden. That is the Mighty Triumph. And another blessing that you love: help from God and a victory near at hand. And give good tidings to the Believers." (Q. 61:10–13)

The graduate from the modern schools would say: "This is a profiteering morality, the morality of the hirelings. It is a base incentive, far beneath doing good for the sake of goodness!"

Such is the objection raised by a morality open to the void, unbelieving in the Hereafter and unfamiliar with the concession granted by God (Glory be to Him) to the True Believers in their progress.

The ideal of doing good for the sake of goodness, and the love of beauty and justice for the sake of beauty and justice, is mere Platonic idealism. It either expresses a stubbornly antireligious attitude, or discloses its frustration and loss in the midst of the materialistic values, the selfish interests and the unscrupulous practices that prevail in a world governed by the policies of domination, and the enslavement of human beings through the internationally legitimized "human rights."

In the bosom of education and purification, the penitent novice is transferred from the love of this world and its charm, and from striving for egoistic pleasure, to the quest for the Hereafter through diligent effort. What a lofty transfer! He is transported from the commerce of this world to the commerce of the Hereafter. What a distance!

It is a concession from the Master (Glory be to Him) Who overlooks the servants' reliance on their deeds, and their dealing with the contract He revealed: "If someone acts thus, he is entitled to such-and-such."

It is hoped that the Generous (Glory be to Him) will raise his servant from this reliance to dependence on His gracious favor (Glory be to Him), mixed with fear of Him and hope in Him. At that stage, the servant sees nothing in himself except shortcoming. With this awareness, he will surely exert himself more strenuously and mobilize all his energies in order to increase in goodness.

At this stage of spiritual progress, the True Believer seeks to be a servant devoted exclusively to God, after his incentive used to be that of a hireling. Excellent indeed is the hireling of the Noble God, Who doubles the good work many times over. Yet His gracious favor is far more extensive and His nearness far more exalted.

From the eye of his heart, at this stage, the reward is concealed. He weeps over his mistakes and his shortcoming, in shame and fear of his Lord. By way of showing gratitude, he begs God for the Garden of Paradise, because God endeared it to us and eloquently described its bounty. Yet his aim is drawing closer to his Lord. The Garden is the destination of those drawn near. Their stations therein are the highest, and the highest bounty is the sight of the Master.

Such a True Believer does now have a favor to ask from God. God's Face has become his final goal and His love his incentive. The straight path to God's contentment and nearness is *jihâd*.

Such a servant, ascending on the ladder of *imân* and *ihsân,* must therefore return to the field of activity. His personal enterprise merges with the enterprise of the community, and his personal Otherworldly aspiration is combined with the collective aspiration for this Afterlife, which we love and of which God's Book gave us the glad tidings:

Help from God and a victory near at hand. (Q. 61:13)

Two Incentives: A Duty and a Right

All goodness is in God's Hand (Glory be to Him) and all evil is unattributable to Him. The True Believer, who is confident in his Lord, is generous with his property and himself, quick to grant rights to their owners. He conceives that as a duty by which he relieves himself of responsibility, and a provision by which he equips himself for his journey to the Hereafter. He never views them as rights snatched from him by human legislation.

The two incentives are not equal: on the one hand, the incentive of the True Believer, who discharges the duty incumbent upon him, and on the other, the incentive of the observer of the prerogatives and sanctions of human legislation.

The system of rights is not identical between the two approaches. The psychological, mental structure is radically different between the believer and the unbeliever.

The community of Muslims and the brotherhood of True Believers are something other than interest-based social, racial, constitutional and national relationships. The former are governed by the rules of the Law that safeguard rights and combat irregularity and deviation. The impetus to sincerity and truthfulness in respecting these rules is the eagerness of the Muslim and the True Believer for their Afterlife, and for the purity of the record with which they will meet their Lord.

We are speaking about the Islam of the truthful, not about the inherited, conventional Islam that is dormant on the lap of indifference.

In the society of brotherly culture that is the goal of aspiration, and that must be preceded by teaching and purification, Muslims will draw their rules of conduct with the international community and the shared environment exclusively from the Qur'an and the *sunna*.

The Emanation of Noble Virtues

From the mosque noble virtues emanate and endeavors become united: one *qibla*,[24] one Qur'an, one will of cooperation and one common burden. The five daily prayers, the Friday congregation and the sermon gather people together. It is a whole system that is not encased within the private self, and an appeal that spreads from neighbor to neighbor.

In the mosque is hoisted the banner of *jihâd*. From its sanctity and its being a gathering place for Muslims, the covenant acquires sanctity and comprehensiveness. Very essential to the active Muslim are truthfulness and knowledge of his rights and duties and what brings him near to God. This is a completely different world from the secularist one! It is not a world that considers methodical doubt to be a noble virtue, chooses egoism as a religion, and revolves around the positive law that is based on the assumption that there is no Deity and no Hereafter, no fear except of your inability to snatch your right, and no hope except for your ability to impose your will.

From the mosque the True Believers emerge, each one having contracted a covenant with God and with his or her brothers and sisters in faith. They have a special nighttime, a special daytime, a special contract and a special brotherhood. Their word is true, their agreement is a firm resolve, their *shûrâ* is an obligation, and their obedience to their leadership is derived from their obedience to God and His Messenger.

In the company of the True Believers, if you sow truthfulness, you reap truthfulness. But if you sow doubt, you reap a whirlwind of doubt, and accumulated doubt leads inevitably to unbelief and its consequences.

And whoever brings the truth and believes therein, such are the dutiful. They shall have whatever they will in the presence of their Lord. That is the reward of the good. (Q. 39:33, 34)

Bound by that sacred covenant with God and the mutual pact between them as a community, the True Believers emerge from the mosque with a resolute will to free, honor and endear Islam to the human being.

With the hoisted banner and the contracted covenant, they emerge to restore Muslims to the Prophetic Method—the Method of the Purifier, the Teacher, the Parent (God bless him and give him peace). They emerge to reunite the *umma,* to acquire means of strength, to bring up the future generations in strength, trustworthiness and *jihâd*. They emerge to share the world's fortunes and misfortunes, to embrace the human being with the kindness of the missionary and the generosity of those who prepare for their Afterlife and hope, by doing so, to win God's mercy and nearness to Him.

Human Dignity

The True Believers bring out to the world the glad tidings:

And We have indeed honored the Children of Adam. (Q. 17:70)

They adhere to the duties of human dignity in its generalities and particulars. The first of those duties, and the most sacred that honors the human being, is God's exclusive worship. In the court of Rustam, the leader of the Persians in the first era, one of the Muslims engaged in *jihâd* said: "God has sent us to bring forth whomever He will from the worship of human divinities to the worship of God, from the hardship of this world to its welfare, and from the tyranny of religions to the justice of Islam."

This statement was uttered by a soldier from the army of a nascent and potent force. The world will only hear this statement from us if we become strong by God's help, by our unity and by the establishment of an exemplary brotherly community that inspires people with its purity, justice, prosperity and utmost care for human dignity.

Our statement must be exemplary, attractive, inviting, liberating, and manifest in an entity that is united, so that the Islamic *umma* may become one as God commanded. It must emanate from the Qur'an and the *sunna,* as a statement that informs every human being of his and her rights. Indeed, it is a statement that is stimulated by faith, not a dictate that is imposed by the strong on the weak.

Good treatment of parents is an imperative duty that comes, in the Qur'anic context, immediately after the duty of the declaration of God's Oneness. What a loss is the lot of those outcasts in old people's homes in civilized Europe and strong and prosperous America!

Giving kinsfolk their due is one of the most imperative duties of brotherly mutual aid. The kinsman has a right. The needy has a right. Whether he begs with his condition or his speech, the beggar has a right.

Give the kinsman his due, and the needy, and the wayfarer. (Q. 17:26)

These gaps in the modern legal and social structure are not filled by the state. They are rather filled by the close, loving and sympathetic hand that draws near, by means of kindness to the people, to the Kind, Gentle, Compassionate Master.

Modern civilization is cold and inhumane. It makes the prosperous increase in egoism, and the wretched in old people's homes and the streets of New York increase in misery.

Paying debts for the indebted is part of *jihâd*. The *umma* is legally indebted. We are imprisoned by the international capitalist law, overwhelmed by foreign debt and usurious interest—a disgraceful mark on humanity's face and a worshipped idol in the temples of the modern era.

Interest, the payment of interest, borrowing for the payment of interest and interest on interest, and the conditions of the IMF and World Bank are highly respected and highly honored articles in the United Nations' Charter.

Money squandering is the work of the devils. Add to it the devilry and usurious interest of capitalism and you find the proportion of the bankruptcy of the underdeveloped peoples, with Muslims in the forefront. Many rulers of the underdeveloped countries have deposits in the banks of usurious civilization equal to the debts of their countries.

Squandering and the misappropriation of Muslims' wealth are harder than successive natural catastrophes. Recovery of the *umma*'s body is impossible, so long as it is bled white by such practices.

The requirements of Islam include speaking well to the human being, bringing up children in kindness and care, and teaching them the principles of faith and chivalry.

One of the rights and duties of human beings is that every man and woman is accountable for those under his or her charge.

Mutual enjoining of what is right and proper and condemning what is wrong and improper are a duty and a right.

Shûrâ and justice are a compulsory prescription.

Kindness to those you know and those you do not know is a lofty virtue, whether they be human beings or any living creatures. In the Prophet's Tradition, a man entered Paradise thanks to a dog whose thirst he quenched, and a woman entered Hell because of a cat she deprived.

Among the Islamic duties is the condemnation of what is wrong and improper and mutual assistance in fighting it.

"Do not associate partners with God. Ascribing partners to Him is a tremendous wrong." (Q. 31:13)

Such is the first advice Muslims must give to one another. Then do not disobey your parents, do not commit perjury, do not flee from the battlefield, do not squander, do not lie, and do not be hypocritical.

Do not kill the soul that God has made sacred, except by way of justice and law. Do not commit adultery and fornication. Do not approach indecencies whether apparent or secret. Do not approach the property of the orphan except to improve it (until he attains the stage of full strength). Do not fail to give measure and weight with full justice. Do not use double-standard policy, for that is unlawful.[25]

> Your Lord has decreed that you must not worship any but Him, and to be good to parents. (Q. 17:23)

From these sacred principles begins the responsibility of every Muslim and the true Muslim state, by reading in the Qur'an and the *sunna* what God prescribed for everyone with regard to responsibilities, duties, individual and collective obligations, justice, *ihsân*,[26] *shûrâ*, brotherhood and mutual compassion between human beings.

That is a sacred reading of sacred duties. In this world where politics is given priority over morality, those politicians who call for morality and human rights are hypocritical opportunists. Men and women of integrity and morality among them are marginalized.

The Islamic wisdom, lost and sought, responds to the question: "How can the conscience of Muslims meet with the morality of men and women of integrity and good will in the world? How is the hand of truthfulness to be extended among all those who are virtuous and free?"

Imam Umar ibn al-Khattab (may God be well pleased with him) was cautious and alert. He used to say: "I am not an impostor, and an impostor would not deceive me." This is one of the answers to the question. God is the One from Whom help is sought!

A History and a Record

The United States of America, supporter of human rights, arms itself with international legitimacy, the unconditional support of the Security Council and the world-wide morality of virtue, in order to impose by force on the underdeveloped nations its point of view and the fulfillment of its own interests.

In the case of Palestine, the United States regards as a right the occupation of its territories and the expulsion of its people by the Jews. It also regards as a right the extermination of Muslims in Bosnia and Herzegovina by the Serbs. It has intervened in Palestine for the last forty-five years to complete the work of British colonialism, while it left the savage Serbs to carry out the carnage in Bosnia.

The Gulf War and the burning of Iraq have demonstrated those rights that the world's military superpower does not permit to be touched: Arab oil, its price control, and the protection of the standard of living of the revered individual American. Let the children of Iraq and the people of Iraq die, as a sacrifice for the sake of the Emir's throne and America's oil!

Arab lands, from the Gulf to the Atlantic, are one American protectorate. That is a bitter reality in the state of human rights.

In the preceding pages, we have been setting forth a record of ethical virtues because our practical record is disgracefully pale. That person who stood confident and audacious in the court of Rustam, to teach Persians and the whole world that God had sent him to bring His servants from the worship of human idols to the worship of God alone— did he have an arsenal to match the forces of the two mighty empires of that era?

He did not have the fighting spirit and organization of Persians, nor the trained legions of Rome. He had ethical virtues and faith in God (Almighty and Glorious is He). He graduated from the mosque, contracted a covenant with God in the mosque and conveyed the Message to the world, waving over his head a banner hoisted in the mosque.

Almighty God made of him and his *umma* a glorious record in the history of humankind. The Muslims were not oppressors or tyrants, because the Qur'an was their thought and its law was their system. Their Islamic incentive was the spiritual strength that represents the difference between the material strength of armies and the dauntless soldier fighting for God's cause.

In our own time, there is an enormous difference between the material strength of a superpower and a scattered and weakened *umma*. So long as we measure by material standards alone, and use imported solutions for our salvation, the gap will even be wider and human rights will only remain a mask that hides our ordeal and defeat.

Two Clashes

Ever since their emergence, the Muslim mind and body have clashed with the other mind and body. That clash had ebbs and flows. Sometimes the other mind and body were in such a state of weakness and agony that you could not speak of any clash, because a living being does not clash with dead entities.

Sometimes our mind and body were in such a state of weakness and stagnation that one could not speak of any confrontation, but could only describe the situation as the Prophet (God bless him and give him peace) described it when he said: "Nations are soon going to rush toward you, as insatiable eaters rush toward a delicious meal." Someone asked: "Will that be due to our being few on that day?" He replied (God bless him and give him peace): "No indeed, you will be numerous on that day, but you will be like the scum of the flood. God will surely remove respect for you from the breasts of your enemy and instill feebleness in your hearts." Someone asked: "O Messenger of God! What is feebleness?" He said (God bless him and give him peace): "Love of this world and dislike of death."[27]

We have become scummy in mind and body, invaded and utterly consumed by civilized and industrial nations that love this life, possess sciences and technology, hate to die and yet put people to death. As for us, we are eager to live any life, however miserable, and we hate physical death, while accepting the death of our dignity and human nature.

The constant clash had two climaxes: First, when the Muslims emerged and marched in the court of Rustam, the land of the Persians and the colonies of Byzantium, they uttered that liberating declaration for which military power opened the space of action, and the mind-liberating declaration of Truth opened the breasts of the nations. In the second climax, the clash began two centuries ago, with the conquest in which the other mind acquired superiority and brought about the dreadful current consequences. What happened to the first Muslim mind, which had a simple culture and a modest understanding of the world, when it entered the countries of others?

That is a necessary question, because the impact of Islam's emergence and its clash with other civilizations, mentalities and philosophies are still manifest today.

We cannot know what "human" and "rights" mean for us and others, unless we make a comparison between the evolution of the Muslim mind and the other mind, leading to their current situation.

From our source and theirs, we ought to observe the most important historical phases of the two minds, until the phase wherein trends and contradictions between the two entities reached the point where coexistence was imposed willy-nilly.

The simple mind, emerging from the mosque into the world, had inevitably to face challenges and questions posed by the contemporary civilizations, the religious philosophies, the idolatrous philosophy, the Roman and Persian presence, and the responsibility of running a nascent empire in full expansion.

What the simple-minded accepted spontaneously had to be evidenced rationally and logically to the arguing nations, whose common folk received liberating Islam with open arms. Muslims encountered resistance particularly from the Jewish rabbis, the Christian monks, the Greek philosophers, the Sabians and the troublemakers among the adepts of Zoroastrianism, Manichaeism, Mazdakism, who protested, argued, conspired and defended their beliefs and their existence.

The centers of resistance were in Syria, the cradle of Hellenistic culture, Harran in Iraq, and Magian Persia.

Islam was victorious in the battlefield, and it quickly gained popularity among peoples of different races from the borders of China to North Africa.

After the political victory, it was essential to incorporate the peoples, to codify the Law, to establish the methods of sciences, to civilize the nomads, to teach the illiterates and to respond to the opposition.

It was essential to prove that the Muslim mind is not at variance with Revelation, and to brandish the weapon of polemics in the face of the sects and creeds that sprang up within the Muslim society, like the Kharijites, or in the centers of resistance where religion was a philosophy and philosophy a religion.

The Muslim mind interacted, learned, incorporated and borrowed. Was it the sun of Aristotelian philosophy that illuminated the path for the Arabic mind until it acquired the status we know?

Did the settlement of the Islamic capital in Roman Damascus, and then in the Iraq of the Chosroes have an effect on the establishment of Umayyad partisanship and then the Abbasid political dynasty based on autocratic rule? Or did the Muslim mind learn social segregation and arrogance as new shading added to its original tribalism? In short, what was the effect of the clash with other cultures on Muslim thinking and Muslim politics?

At present, we are faced with the same question and the same challenge, though with a large difference: In their encounter with Greek philosophy, Eastern religions, Indian sciences, Persian Chosroeism and Roman Caesarism, the Muslims were the strong ones. Today, we are outweighed and in a weak condition.

The current challenge tells us this: We cannot survive, in a world of fierce competition and hegemonic superpowers, without development, technology, financial resources, military power, political stability, social harmony, combined efforts and mobilization. None of that can be achieved without rationalizing thought and politics. In other words, there is no way out except by rejecting Islam, and by adopting the materialist religion and the system of secular democracy that casts religion into the far corner.

Our purpose from the beginning has been to follow the secular argument, in order to refute the "modernist" claims. We wish to prove that the rule based on *shûrâ* and the religious mind, learning without impediments from the Book of God and the wisdom of the world, can alone insure life, strength, development, growth and unity for Muslims.

In the first era and over many centuries, the philosophizers among Muslims strove to integrate religion into philosophy and philosophy into religion. From al-Kindi, al-Farabi and Ibn Sina (Avicenna) to Ibn Tufail and Ibn Rushd (Averroës), the philosophizing motto was: "Directing the Law toward wisdom." Such was the formula of their integrative secularism. Today, the secularism of our contemporaries is separatist, in that it wants religion to be confined to the private sphere, while the public sphere is left to politics.

All roads lead to secularism!

For their part, the Islamic jurists used to insist that the Islamic sources of legislation, the Qur'an and the *sunna,* were not in conflict with what is comprehended by means of reasoning.

From the free-will Mu'tazilites, who disputed the Illuminist philosophy and Greek logic, to Ibn Taimiya, who disputed the Mu'tazilites and all the sects—passing by al-Ghazali, who fought the esotericists—the Muslim scholars endeavored to present Islam as it originally was: a perfect religion that appoints the mind as a servant of Revelation.

Imam al-Ghazali (may God bestow His mercy upon him) represents the open mind that seeks perfection and knocks at every door, wherever it thinks to find a lamp by which it will be illuminated.

Armed with his Legistic weapon, he argued with philosophers and demonstrated their absurdity. That was considered an offense, for which our present philosophers will not forgive him. They consider him a model of Islamic thought's obscurantism, and describe his affiliation with the Sufis as unbelief, an adoption of Harranian, Sabian and Illuminist philosophy, and a proof of the nonchalance and indifference that afflicted the Muslim mind.

Al-Ghazali used the mental weapon of Legistic theologians. He believed that Theology and its deductive methods did not conflict with Aristotelian logic. In his books, he expressed admiration for Definition and Proof—two principles regarded by Aristotle as the summit of knowledge. His contemporaries defamed him for that, as did the scholars after them, especially Shaikh al-Islam Ibn Taimiya.

About the methods of Greek logic, he said in the introduction to his book al-Maqâsid:[28] "Most of them are right and the errors they bear are few. They differ with the holders of the Truth (the Muslims) in terminology, not in objectives. Their purpose is the refinement of deductions, which is a feature that all men of logic share."

Apart from al-Ghazali in the first stages of his research, and some scholars who came after him, Muslim scholars generally rejected Greek logic. They fought the heretical doctrines and the novel philosophies with the weapon of Analogy/Syllogism and its tools.

The first to reject the Aristotelian Greek logical tool was the genius of the scholars, Imam ash-Shafi'i (may God be well pleased with him), the founder of the Science of the Roots [of Islamic Law]. The scholars who came after him did the same, because Greek logic rests on materialistic physics and metaphysics, which are two subjects conflicting with the Islamic creed, just as the language of the Greeks is conflicting with the language of the Qur'an.

They rejected the tool because they rejected the content. Can an imported tool ever be safe from inherent germs? They developed a logic that took advantage of what "is shared by all men of logic." After being islamicized, the subject was instructed in the mosque alongside Grammar, Jurisprudence, Exegesis of the Qur'an, the Prophetic Tradition and the rest of the sciences. They criticized the Greek logical tool because it was based on theoretical inferential methodology, whereas Muslim thinking is based on investigation and experimentation.

The Science of the Roots, Jurisprudence, Linguistics and Grammar gained a great advance through their reliance on the Muslim methodological tool. Instead of the Aristotelian Definition and Proof, these sciences employed Legistic Analogy with its tool and its doctrine in probing, classification and the other rules of the Science of the Roots.

Probing and classification are an experimental methodology that proceeds through classifying the subject into details, examining the shared features and the common causes, making a profound criticism of the particulars (that is probing) and gradually discarding the probabilities that are not verifiable by experimentation.

No matter how disputation became intense between Muslims, mutual tolerance was the prevailing feature. The philosophers lived in safety. No Bruno among them was burned to death, and no Galileo was put on trial before a Holy Office. Al-Kindi, al-Farabi and Ibn Sina, then Ibn Baja (Avempace), Ibn Tufail and Ibn Rushd were not persecuted. The jurists looked askance at them, the scholars of *Hadîth*[29] scowled in their faces and all scholars, generation after generation, argued with them and refuted their arguments. But no gallows were erected and no stakes were set alight.

Did Aristotelian logic liberate the Muslim mind? Was Ibn Rushd with his new pure Aristotelianism the stimulator of Europe's Renaissance? If so, then let us be Aristotelians with Rushdian authenticity, in order to liberate ourselves and join the leading countries! Aristotle's liberating philosophy, as Ibn Rushd dispatched it to Europe, was the pillar of the Church's greatest philosopher, Thomas Aquinas. We all know what freedom the Church practiced!

As for the authenticity for which we have a vital need, it is the recovery of the empirical methodology that was born from the womb of our Legistic Analogy and that others claim to be theirs.

We shall take the basic formula considered as the key to the exact sciences[30] from the statement of a well-established authority in the domain, the renowned scientist in the sciences of light and Optics, the teacher of the generations and the initiator of the path pursued by Galileo, Newton and Bacon. That key is unfortunately held hostage by the scientific mind that rules the world.

The man in question is Ibn al-Haitham, who said: "We embark on research with the investigation of existing entities, scrutinizing the conditions of the things observed by the eye and the distinction of the particulars. Then, we investigate by means of perception the peculiarities of sight, what is constant and what is visible."

He went on to say: "Then we advance, gradually and sequentially, in research and measurement while reviewing the premises and making reservations about the results. We make our investigation and scrutiny abide by the principles of objectivity, not biased judgment, and by the search for the truth, not blind imitation of opinions. . . . Perhaps we shall finally attain by this method, based on gradual progress, careful criticism and making reservations, to the indisputable truth that removes all doubts."

I quoted him (may God bestow His mercy upon him) from the book *Manâhij al-Bahth inda Mufakkiri'l-Islam*[31] by Dr. Ali an-Nashshar, who, in his turn, quoted from Mustafa Nazif (may God bestow His mercy upon them all).

The current Arab and other philosophers do not concede that this brilliant and splendid methodology sprang from the Science of the Roots. The admiration for "what is shared by all men of logic," which they find in the books of Ibn al-Haitham, is similar to that found in the books of al-Ghazali.

It is not important to find whether or not there is a link between empiricism and Aristotelianism. The most important point is this: The statement we have read was fashioned by a Muslim mind that did not feel a need to reject religion in order to make progress, because it was not a vanquished mind but rather a victorious mind.

History belies the false connection between the father Aristotle and the mother Bacon. (There are two Bacons: Francis and Roger, to both of whom the empirical procedure is attributed.)

If Ibn Rushd was any mediator, he was surely the instructor of the Church in the person of its son, Thomas Aquinas.

Roger Bacon, to whom the empirical procedure is attributed, was an Englishman prominent in the sciences of his time. He studied in Andalusia[32] and was one of the messengers of the sciences. He took them with their empirical tools to many countries and nations. He never ceased throughout his life to express his gratitude to whom it was due. According to an English scholar, he maintained that "the knowledge and science of the Arabs are the unique path to the knowledge of the Truth."[33]

The English scholar proved that Roger Bacon made a profound study of Arab sciences and that no credit is due to him, nor to his namesake Francis Bacon, for the discovery of the empirical method in Europe.

The fair witness said that Roger Bacon was, in fact, only one of the messengers of the sciences and the Islamic empirical method to Christian Europe. Roger Bacon never ceased to declare that the knowledge and sciences of the Arabs were the unique path to true knowledge. He used to reiterate that declaration to his contemporaries.

The European witness then mentioned that there were many debates about the founders of the empirical method, and that they were based on a false and distorted depiction of the sources of Europe's civilization.

He said that the true source of European civilization was the empirical method of the Arabs, which spread in the era of Bacon and was keenly learned by the people of Europe.

He added that the most important influence of Islamic culture on European science was on "natural science and the scientific spirit, which are the two distinctive features of modern science and the two lofty sources of its flourishing."

The European witness also testified "that what our science owes to the science of the Arabs is not what they presented to us from their discovery of novel and active theories. Science is indebted to Arabic culture for more than that. . . . It is indebted to it for its very existence. . . . Astronomy and Greek mathematics were foreign elements that found no suitable place in Greek culture."

He said: "The methods of research and the gathering and concentration of positive knowledge, the subtle methods of science, the profound and detailed examination and empirical research were all alien to the Greek temperament. . . . What we call science appeared in Europe as a result of the new spirit of research and new procedures of investigation . . . , experimentation, examination and Analogy, and as a result of the development of mathematics in a form unknown to the Greeks. Such spirit and such methods were introduced by the Arabs into the European world."

Now that I have finished quoting his speech, I shall correct two statements. The first is the term science in the singular. Science in the singular is the perfect science—the knowledge of God, the human being and his ultimate destiny. Its source is Revelation, to which human thought has no access except by means of the Messengers (Peace be upon them). As for what human thought acquires by the means deposited in it from the exact sciences, it is appropriate to refer to them as sciences in the plural.

The second correction is that these sciences were not referred to as Arabic sciences in Andalusia, Baghdad, Damascus or Qairawan.[34] Their Arabic language was the language of the Muslims. They were therefore Islamic sciences without any racial qualification. In them participated the geniuses of the Islamic peoples, including Arabs, Persians, Turks, Afghans, Berbers, half-castes and the rest of the Muslim non-Arab peoples, who adopted the Arabic language just as they embraced Islam as a religion.

Furthermore, Andalusia, whose light shone over Europe, was the cradle of geniuses in Astronomy, Mathematics and Medicine, not that of the philosophers and their precursor, Ibn Rushd.

Perhaps Rushdism, whose thinking had invaded Europe for centuries, was a pioneer in its fundamental rejection of the insertion of religion into philosophy, and in "directing the Law toward wisdom." Perhaps pure Aristotelian Rushdism (only Aristotle!) taught Thomas Aquinas the logical deduction that the religion of the Church is true, and taught the progeny that gave birth to Voltaire and the philosophy of the Enlightenment that religion ought not to enter into philosophy, nor philosophy into religion.

Rushdism, celebrated like the Mu'tazilite thought by the contemporary Arab philosophers, was thus a pioneer in two spheres, a teacher of two arts. Perhaps it was the doctrine by which the Church became well established in the world of obscurantist, intolerant and reactionary thought, and by which the slaves of the Church liberated themselves from the yoke of the Church.

The contemporary Arab philosophers search for a predecessor in secularism. Thus they invoke the specter of Ibn Rushd and search among the Mu'tazilites for original fathers of audacious rationalism.

By the way, why should we perform postmortem examination of stiff corpses? Aristotelian philosophy is dead and gone. Other subsequent philosophies equally died, refuted as they were by the advance of the sciences. Whenever the scientific mind discovers a new horizon of knowledge, the philosophic mind sees its original horizon eclipsed. Whenever the discoveries establish a new continent for the sciences, the edifice of philosophy collapses. Then philosophy seeks the help of its brother— the scientific mind—in order to erect a new structure.

Philosophies have died and still die. They have declared bankruptcy and they still do so. Their inquiries about the mysteries of existence have been, and will always be, fruitless. They have banged their head on the brick wall of enigmas and the questions that *fitra* asks about principles, reasons and meaning. They ended up making their head bleed. Metaphysics has failed to provide a single convincing answer.

Philosophy was declared bankrupt and incompetent when the empirical mind posed questions for which it had no answer. It stacked these questions and classified them in the stores of the unknown, and put on them the label "Parapsychology." It acted as if classifying unknown things, compiling encyclopedias about what the human being does not know, and attaching pompous labels, were a science and an achievement of knowledge.

The science of Galileo, descending directly from the astronomers of Andalusia, established for Descartes and his generation a platform on which he built his fame. He founded the methodology of doubt and trust in the mind of "I think, therefore I am," in order to prove the existence of God. The Cartesians soon seized the principle of doubt and trust in the reasoning of the mind, in order to combat the existence of metaphysics above sensory perception. Descartes' methodologi‹ losophy died, despite the importance of his scientific achievements.

As we have read earlier, Roger Bacon transmitted the methodology of Muslims to the English, for whom it reinforced the spirit of pragmatism expressed by Locke and Hume. They began to believe only in what they have seen and touched, and they turn with every wind that brings rain.

Newton's physics provided a basis for Kant's philosophy, and inspired it with confidence in the rebellious mind around which everything revolves, just as the planets revolve around the sun.

Kant's philosophy died when Planck's quantum physics and Einstein's theory of relativity arose at the dawn of the 20th century. The philosophies that built their glory on the scientists of this century multiplied, were dispersed and clashed with one another. They are doomed to die with the latest fashion in the world of sciences: the theory of cosmic chaos.

Sciences used to have confidence in their discoveries. Today, they are aware that what they have produced today will flee from them tomorrow. Determinism and order in the universe were the two signs that God (Almighty and Glorious is He) disclosed to this exploring, investigating mind. Today, He has disclosed to it that there is no Determinism and no order. The researcher is left behind his microscope awaiting the elements of the atom. Will they come to the rendezvous or fail to show up? Will they appear in waves and rays as energy appears, or will they come fragmented as in the case of matter?

Ordered chaos, mysteries in the universe, and what a great mystery dwells in you, O human being!

Coming Back Home!

At the end of this survey, we come out with the following: Did the Muslims who formulated scientific methodology abandon their Islam? Did they divorce the Muslim mind from its proper functions? Or did they excel in the sciences because of their firm commitment to Science?

By means of the same Legistic Analogy, adapted to the subject [since it is one of the "Roots" or basic principles of Islamic jurisprudence], they commenced their understanding of God's revealed Law and their research in God's created universe.

It is true that the affliction on the mind was severe, suffocating and deadly. The assault came from those tyrannical regimes that locked the door of *ijtihâd*[35] and muzzled people's mouths, so that no one would say anything other than what the ruler said. The Abbasid al-Ma'mun said: "Be Mu'tazilites!" The Mu'tazilite doctrine reigned supreme and the backs of the leading scholars were whipped.

The reasoning mind was smothered in our lands. So its scientific spirit flew away. It settled in the other countries, since it did not find in the lands of the Muslims any shelter, any nursery, any care and protection.

How shall we convince the scientific mind to come back to its land of origin? At what price shall we lodge the scientific spirit in the Muslim society?

The answer is self-evident: The scientific mind will not come back home, so long as the culprits who choke freedoms and violate human rights are in power.

It will not come back without an unrelenting struggle. Over there, it is held hostage and kept under tight surveillance by sentries who have installed it in secure custody.

Their agents among us are haggling over the ransom: You have no access to it unless you embrace the religion of the foster parents. Be secularists like them. The other conditions are open to discussion.

Dumps . . . and Dumps

The other conditions are difficult, because the elements of the adoptive civilization are replete with the relics of intellectual history and its head-splitting philosophical dumps, which have stacked up against Islam.

According to the Greek roots of Western material idolatry: The human being is for Art, so join our arts! They also declare: The human being is a successor on earth to Prometheus, the stealer of fire from the gods of Olympus. So be with us as tyrants on earth! Accept the esthetics of the Greeks, the worshipped woman, the worshipped body, physical exercise and the Olympian fantasy.

The Jewish sources deeply rooted in Western civilization state: For God's Chosen People there is no objection to despising the gentile (goy, pl. *goyîm* in Hebrew), cheating him and usurping his money and property by means of usury and trickery. The colored gentile is entitled to be content with whatever is thrown to him. O Palestine, who is your Saladin?

As far as might is concerned, Athenian racist democracy and Roman imperialistic rigid law subscribe to the Jewish theory of the gentile.

Likewise, unscrupulous Machiavellianism, according to which the end justifies the means, agrees with the theory in terms of both might and cunning.

Materialist philosophy, which lies in one of the geological strata of Western culture, declares: The human being is an intellectual evolution that has outgrown the infancy of the religions. He is entitled to study the liberating sciences, provided that his neighbor from among God's Chosen People does not object.

Existentialism puts forward: The human being is an absurdity thrown into the universe. He is entitled to amusement, despairing grief and suicide, or engagement in a Marxist class struggle by which the human being makes for himself an honorable existence.

Darwinism, established in the cultural geology, asserts that: The human being is an evolved ape, entitled to practice his bestiality with freedom, spontaneity and struggling competition. His axiom is: Survival for the strongest and death for the weakest. The fittest is the strong animal happy to be an ape.

For Agnostics: The human being is an unintelligible enigma. He is entitled to metaphysical suffering.

Atheism declares from its stratum: The human being is a cog in the waterwheel of life. He is entitled to seize the opportunity of his short life.

The economist doctrine maintains that: The human being is one of the basic resources. He is entitled to perform his functional duty.

According to Marxism: The human being is a factor of production. Either he turns the wheel or else he is dragged off to the Gulag.

For Capitalism: The human being is a market and a consumer. He is entitled to have goods made highly attractive by the advertising and canning industry.

The sexual revolution advances that: The human being is a tool for pleasure. He is entitled to sex without limits. Adultery and fornication are words not to be uttered, because they are obsolete relics.

Nietzsche says: The human being is for the mighty. The weak have no right to life.

Freud stipulates that: The human being is sudden moods. He is imbued with desires in his wakefulness as well as in his sleep. He is not to be restrained or prevented from satisfying his desires.

According to the love of pomp in a crazy world: Setting records is the value of the human being, his right and his duty—be that in sports or wolfing down the greatest quantity of eggs in the shortest time.

From the innermost recesses, Nationalism states that: The human being is who I am, and my nation state is my life and my death, my war and my peace. As for the peoples that have not been destroyed by the two World Wars, and have not been taught the necessity of being united by the Cold War and the conflict of the Superpowers, they are to enjoy being peculiar dwarf countries, stagnating in poverty and fighting other peoples. They are to worship the nation state as the monks worship the Cross, and arm themselves until they become conquering Serbs, exterminated Bosnians, or Somalis relieved by the U.N.'s human rights organizations, after half of them have starved to death and the other half have been killed in tribal conflict.

The collective memory, which has not forgotten what Saladin did to the Eastern Kingdom of the Franks, prescribes that: Islam is the enemy. The right of the world against the Muslim human being, who is proud to be Muslim, is to rally international intelligence agencies against him, and hold conferences in order to combat and eliminate his terrorism.

The humble collective conscience was rebuked by the Jewish propaganda about the inflated number of God's Chosen People massacred by Hitlerism. The Church also apologized: The Jewish human being is your true brother. You must protect him as you protect yourselves, supply him with weapons and disclose nuclear secrets to him.

In the collective memory reverberates the echo of the collapse of the Byzantine Empire in Constantinople at the hand of Muhammad II the Conqueror. There also reverberates the echo of the siege laid by the Turkish Muslim soldiers to Vienna. The word *jihâd*—in the Western collective memory—is a disturbing and savage word that deserves to be erased from all dictionaries!

The specter of colonization looms up before the *jihâd* of the Muslims to expel colonial troops, the fighting spirit of the Algerian Muslims in their war against France, the revolution of Iran and the Afghan lions,[36] and says: Don't worry! We have left our children, our protégés and our agents at home.

We have been considering the negative aspects of a civilization that is proliferation-oriented, tyrannical, wasteful, satanic and polluting. It has polluted the sky and the earth, the water and the air. It has also polluted the minds with its crazy philosophy.

Comparison . . . and a Comparison

We have judged the faults and effects of philosophy by the standards of the Qur'an. Yet this is not an appropriate measure of comparison.

Comparing our practical faults with their practical virtues makes the proper and balanced comparison, for we are not seeking a verbal revenge or an oral Schadenfreude. We are seeking the way to liberate our minds from the dumps, from what armed colonization brought, what it left in us through associating and mixing with the colonizers, and what we have initially inherited from our traditional faults and diseases.

Huge dumps have accumulated in the depths of our minds and souls. The negative aspects interacted, proliferated and became complicated. Our illness is thus complex.

Our illness is perpetuated and the servitude of our minds is reinforced, because we refuse to acknowledge our own faults. We take pleasure in criticizing others; we shy away from the duty of stern self-confrontation, and we blame the crusading and Zionist conspiracy for our illnesses and our pains.

"You could not have been colonized had you not been colonizable." Thus said Malek ibn Nabi[37] (may God have mercy on him). They would not have left an ignoble progeny appointed to rule in the region, had you not been afflicted with an inherited decadence.

They would not have been able to fill your minds and your lifestyle with their philosophical excretions, their tools of civilization, their consumer goods and their cultural fashions, had you not been an open public market.

Let us then compare their virtues with our faults, in order to see how far we are outdistanced. Only then shall we be entitled to think of the word that the human being is waiting to hear from us concerning his supreme right. He will not hear from us unless we remedy our faults, cure ourselves of our diseases and, through self-discipline first of all, gain virtues and strength.

Skillful weavers will only scoff at a naked person who criticizes their weaving tools, the colors of their clothes, the sources of their cotton, and the economy of their workshops. They will tell him: "Clothe yourself and then come for discussion!"

How shameful is the comparison between the virtues of the skillful

European weavers and our traditional rags and borrowed nakedness! It is even more shameful if we compare our poverty and industrial destitution with Japan's wealth, industry and sciences.

"Just yesterday, you were like us! How did you manage to take the lead in one single century?"

We shall soon be posing the same question to China and all the other nations, as they pass in front of us while we are looking at our useless counterfeit clothes.

Some of Their Virtues

We shall be referring to some of the strong virtues that are deeply rooted in their Western culture, and that are resisting the inherent destructive elements of their moth-eaten civilization. They include:

Freedom, freedom and freedom. They do not acknowledge servitude to God, because they are unbelievers and *jâhilîya*. Yet they are immunized against human autocracy.

Sciences, the fruits of the sciences and spending on scientific research. Conscientiousness and competence in work.

The virtue of being governed by organized schedules, while we are ruled by temperament and improvisation.

The virtue of being governed by planning, initiative and anticipation of results, while we sleep until we are surprised by catastrophes.

Organization and alertness.

Democracy, which turns in our lands into a comedy, a folkloric festival, political rigging and one-upmanship.

Realism that makes them view democracy as the best system available in relation to their civilized background. They use democracy while being aware of its faults, limits and manipulations. For us, it is a mythical and idealistic word, which we place in the pantheon of our impotent and servile dreams.

Civil society with its real party pluralism, active associations, struggling unions, and its humanitarian merits that rush to Somalia to feed our hungry and nurse our wounds.

The law that applies to the strong and the weak. We do not judge them according to the ideal of the Qur'an and the jurisdiction of God, for they are *jâhilîya* who abide by the choice of the people in setting their constitutions and codifying their laws. The result is a legal system that has known results, limits and rights, and that leaves no room for the ruler's absolute will.

A judiciary that is relatively independent.

The citizen who clings to his rights and is able, when offended, to pursue his offender.

The free press that keeps watch, criticizes and even dismisses heads of state who violate privacy, as in Watergate.

The political refugee from us, driven into exile by our oppressive tyrants, finds with them refuge, safety, assistance and humane care. Let that be enough!

Their virtues are as many as our conventional faults and the new defects weakening our Islam and our *umma*.

The Mirror of Our Faults

Their virtues are a negative mirror to our faults. What seems black to us appears there to the abdicator from his religion as pure whiteness.

Let us send the comparison between pure whiteness and pitch-blackness to the world of ideals. Instead, let us focus on our own self with sharp transparency. That is *Nasîha*,[38] which is part of Faith, or rather, it is the essence of Faith.

We apply *nasîha* not for self-flagellation but rather to see how much we are outdistanced in chivalry, and to assess how much effort is required for the reconstruction of the self that is based on the Prophetic Method.

If their racism, born of nationalistic, ethnic, chauvinistic Athenian democracy, is peculiar to the European white man, ours is primitive tribalism. Some tribes swagger in clothes of petroleum, while others are naked. Some clans have seized the properties of Muslims, while others in Bangladesh are destitute. Bellies are inflated from unlawful food, wallowing on beds of debauchery, while the Somalis are dying of hunger before the eyes of the world.

They are distinguished by a cohesive democratic society and continuous rotation of governments, while our rulers are eternal and our society is made of crumbs. They would not have been lifelong rulers, had our *umma* not been a delicious meal. That only indicates the efforts required for reconstruction.

The thinking of others has evolved, while our minds and souls are haunted by sorcery, superstition and the various arts of "sacred religious magic." We are among the outcasts of this world. It is quite useless for us to condemn absurd existentialism, consoling ourselves with the illusion that they have this world and we have the Hereafter. Our Hereafter is hashed and riddled, if we neglect our mission and dwell in this world as outcasts.

We are the monkeys. They come for vacation in our lands, to enjoy our folklore in hotels, casinos, night taverns and night girls. You cannot describe the evils that libertinism inflicts on our men and women. We import AIDS with the blonde tourist whores. There settles in our lands a plague on top of the plague of the dollars that our children beg on tourist streets.

Production, work, conscientiousness and diligence are plants that do not grow in our lands, because of the dominance of such parasitic plants as bribery, favoritism and irresponsibility.

We are a cog in the waterwheel of economic, social and political underdevelopment. What is the point of lamenting over the condition of apish Darwinism and the atheistic vacuum, when you have no industry other than tourism, and your libertine condition says: "This is nothing but our worldly life!"?

We are merely demographic figures, proliferating, scummy, wretched and outcast. We do not know how to take pride in our great numbers among the nations, nor how our Prophet (God bless him and give him peace) can take pride in us while we are scum, carried away by the flood.

We are the supplementary, marginal market. They throw us the surplus of their factories, which pollutes the environment, just as they throw us the toys of their technology and the surplus of their agriculture. Consequently, we consume what we do not manufacture and eat what we do not cultivate.

We are thereby worthless on the heavy international balances.

Shunning the Profession

The medical and nursing profession is shunned by those who lack the courage to examine the suppurating wound, the contagious disease and the prerequisites of the remedy.

If someone supposes that those who come out from the mosque to cleanse society are infallible angels descending from heaven, he will only be immersed in fantasy and delusion.

They are only a part of that society whose symptoms of sickness we have just been stating. They are the sons and daughters of that environment. They purify themselves by means of their strenuous effort in missionary work. They themselves are a subject for remedial treatment during their entrance into the public space.

If the therapist masks his face, so as not to see his patient's real sickness, or views him through rose-colored spectacles, so that his sight is not stained with the color of pus, he is bound to stain his hands and clothes. If the diagnosis is mistaken or distorted, the treatment will be mere sorcery, even if the prescribed medication is generally healing and salutary.

"To God belongs the outcome of affairs!"

A Rotten Civilization

We come out from comparing the shared human chivalry that is absent, suppressed and despised here, while it is present, flourishing and actively practiced over there, so that we may place the comparison in its Islamic perspective, which evaluates the human being and history in the light of faith.

In this perspective, they are *jâhilîya* and we are Muslims. That is an essential difference, because someone who believes in God and the Last Day is not like someone who does not believe. The unbelievers and the *jâhilîya* civilization are superior in the means of strength and the adornment of worldly life, but they remain on the scale of eternity in loss and bankruptcy.

Shaikh Muhammad Abduh (may God bestow His mercy upon him) visited Europe, and after his return was reported as having said: "Over there is Islam without Muslims, and here are Muslims without Islam!"

Was this pioneer dazzled by the material superiority of the smart streets of civilization, by order, industry, sciences, the judicious and well-mannered conduct, the social propriety and the military strength, and all the other virtues?

We recognize those virtues and disclose our faults. We have to make that horizontal earthly comparison, lest we live in dreams, making ourselves see the world as we desire, not as the world is in reality. But Muslims, even if they have neglected their Islam and its virtues, are still Muslims.

The people of *jâhilîya* retain their character, regardless of what they have achieved in material progress, worldly comfort, prosperity, strength and adornment. Unbelief is over there and belief in God and the Last Day is over here. This is an essential distinction. The other differences are accidental.

They are accidental and fortuitous, but decisive. How serious is the difference between them and us, with regard to such material virtues as sciences, chivalry and organization. The strong model is attractive and contrastive, as it sets their virtues against our faults, their strength against our weakness. By so doing, it cripples our Islam.

In a few generations, we may become—God forbid!—merely nominal Muslims, like those Muslims among our offspring who have been ground in the mills of westernization, whose Islam has been obliterated by cultural assimilation. On that day—God forbid!—we may say: "We are Muslims without Islam." But will others have Islam without being Muslims? Is Islam wealth, skyscrapers, external tidiness, atom bombs, sciences, organization and material strength?

No!

Islam is true and *jâhilîya* is false. Whatever the accidental virtues and faults, the former is light and the latter is darkness. I shall take the comparison from the earth to heaven and from worldly life to the eternal scene. Then:

> Let it not delude you, that those who disbelieve enjoy freedom of action in the land. A little enjoyment, but then their habitation will be Hell, an evil cradle! (Q. 3:196, 197)

God's Custom in History

Let not the fascination of *jâhilîya* civilization delude you, for its foundations are gradually moth-eaten. The effect of the rot will become apparent with the passing of time, year after year, and decadence after decadence. After whatever God will, God's Custom in dealing with His servants and His creation will be proclaimed to their iniquitous civilization, as in the Qur'anic verse:

> Those are their dwellings, empty and in ruins, because they did wrong. Surely therein is a sign for a people who know. (Q. 27:52)

That verse was revealed concerning Thamud, the people of Salih (God bless him and give him peace). They had a civilization, gardens, wells, farms, structures, houses and liveliness. Yet they were ungrateful for God's bounties and acted wrongfully. They did not believe their Messenger, and that is the most terrible wrongdoing. God (Exalted is He) said about them:

> So they plotted a plot; and We plotted a plot, while they did not perceive. Then see the nature of the consequence of their plotting, for We destroyed them and their people. (Q. 27:50, 51)

He (Exalted is He) also said about those who believed in His Messenger Salih (Peace and prayer be upon him):

> And We saved those who believed and used to practice true devotion. (Q. 27:53)

In dealing with the unbelievers, His cunning device was to let them enjoy themselves for a while, leaving them to wallow in their sins and providing them with wealth and progeny. Then He seized them with His mighty grasp (Exalted is He).

Such is His Custom (Exalted is He): He causes the days to rotate among people, He establishes the proof against the sinful wrongdoers who turn away from their Lord, then He destroys them. He said (Glorious is He):

> How many a township have We destroyed while it was sinful, so that it lies in ruins, and a deserted well and lofty tower. (Q. 22:45)

Such are signs for people who know and practice true devotion! Knowledge includes awareness of His Custom (Exalted is He), while true devotion includes repentance to Him (Glory be to Him) and returning to His Custom and the Method of His Prophet, as well as gathering the strength to receive His Mercy, which says:

> The earth shall be the inheritance of My righteous servants. (Q. 21:105)

The civilization of atom bombs is an iniquitous civilization. This is an announcement of its ruination, whenever God will. Whatever worldly property it has amassed has no value, except insofar as we are tested with destitution while they are stuffed to the full, with poverty while they are rich, with weakness while they are strong, and with fragmentation while they are united in conspiracy against us.

From behind their stockpile, we glimpse the manifestation of God's Custom in cunning, indulgence and testing, as clearly expressed in His saying (Exalted is He):

> And were it not that humankind would have become one community, We might well have appointed for those who disbelieve in the All-Merciful, roofs of silver for their houses and stairs for them to mount, and doors for their houses and couches whereon to recline, and ornaments of gold. Yet all that would have been but a provision of the life of this world, and the Hereafter with your Lord would have been for the truly devout. (Q. 43:33–35)

Then, after finding right guidance in God's Custom as conveyed by Revelation, we contemplate God's treatment of His servants as conveyed by Fate.

The floor of this unjust civilization—guilty of injustice in every sense, especially the monstrous injustice of unbelief—is fissured. Its walls are rotten. Its philosophical foundation is flimsy, trivial and bestial. Its structure is cracked. The tidiness of the streets of Geneva and Paris conceals the filthiness of morality and the cancer of libertinism.

The sweepings of this wasteful, extravagant civilization spread the plague of pollution, especially in the underdeveloped regions.

Its cultural, artistic, cynical, naked, dancing, crazy sweepings cover the globe through their televised broadcasting, which kills humanity in the human being.

Narcotics, crime, violence, coldness of human relationships, shameless egoism, licensed adultery, fornication and homosexuality, family breakup—the list is very long.

The inheritors are knocking at the door. Once the Muslims are quali-

82

fied to inherit the earth, God's Custom is an unbroken promise and the conditions of qualification are well known.

That may be in a century or two, or less or more than that. Maybe when God (Almighty and Glorious is He) will have revolved power on earth between two or more *jâhilîya* poles. Maybe after the turn of Japan, Europe, China, and what God alone knows.

Or God may employ Japan, China, America, France, Germany, or any of the people of the time He wishes, to convey the Message of Islam after they have received it from us. The Tartars, who pillaged Baghdad and stacked the skulls of the scholars in heaps, were no less barbaric and destructive than the burners of Baghdad and the deserters of Bosnia in our own age. The Tartars then embraced Islam and became one of its strongest guardians. Islamic expansion and guidance have already begun among individual members of those peoples. The mission will become a serious and general matter whenever God will, when the missionary is prepared and has learned the skill of weaving before he enters the weavers' clubhouse. Those who are clothed do not hear the speech of the naked.

The Kernel of History

W hatever it may be, the journey has begun. Whatever the long ride may be, the caravan is on the move. The Islamic awakening is not an illusory flash of lightning—God forbid! It is not a mere fairy tale—we pin our hope on God! "Success comes only from God."

The Prophetic Method gives glad tidings of a Caliphate based on the Prophetic Method after centuries of despotic rule. The Prophetic Method is universal in its mission and strength, and it is God's guidance for creatures.

The western civilization will eventually collapse, even if it lasts for a while. Meanwhile, a nascent power is gaining strength by the grace of God, the Lord of the universe (Glorified be He).

Nevertheless, the preconditions remain unchanged and our sickness must be remedied. The obligations must be fulfilled, because God's Custom favors no one nor makes him an exception. The door will be slammed in our face, if we knock with the pretension of those who have righteous predecessors and belong to a blessed *umma,* surrounded with God's compassion and solicitude, while not being qualified to inherit. We shall be driven away if we come to obtain the reward but have not worked, have not competed, and have not done our utmost.

By obeying God and following the Method of His Prophet, we shall succeed triumphantly. The balance of power according to which we are nothing ought not to frustrate our resolution.

After a period of time, you will examine the result of history, or read God's Custom henceforth in His saying (Exalted is He):

How many a generation have We destroyed before them, who were more imposing in gear and outward appearance! (Q. 19:74)

—and His saying:

And how many a generation before them have We destroyed! Can you see a single man among them, or hear from them the slightest sound?" (Q. 19:98)

It is a serious mistake for the assaulted Muslim mind to read history and view the future from a material perspective. That is the manifestation of the influence of *jâhilîya* thinking, which is heedless of God and of God's Custom, on the thinking of the Muslims. The canals of the orientalist thought have been spilled into our minds by the Westernized elite. The programs of colonial education have made history superficial in our eyes. We perceive its past and future only as a struggle between people, a balance of power, a life without a Hereafter, a competition between winners and losers, and a meaningless effort on earth for an absurd human being and an outcast humanity.

The educational programs handed over by the *jâhilîya* foreigners have exaggerated the setbacks of the political history of Muslims and their internal struggles. On the other hand, they have concealed the history of faith, the continuity and rightness of Islam and the triumph of the successful.

The history of faith, Islam, righteousness and success has been consigned to the scrap heap. It has been ridiculed and treated as meaningless prattle in the language of people who do not believe in God nor in the Last Day.

The materialist historian seduces his Islamic disputant, and casts him out of the territory of perfection into that of disconnection. Consequently, he indulges in comparing Islam's might and worldly possessions with those of the other, while being forgetful of God's Custom, the kernel and meaning of existence.

It is like someone who takes the train for a precise destination. His long stay with the other passengers makes him forget the destination; the world becomes for him confined to the passengers in the train; he gets so involved in conversation that he totally forgets that he is on a journey.

Common ground and shared virtues are a common factor, a fate and a trial, a profit or a deficit.

The questions that must be asked are: What are we? Where are we going? Whence do we come?

On the lands of the *jâhilîya* people, numerous skyscrapers have been erected. The atomic sciences are a horrible force, electronics and computer science are a baffling vortex, and the breakthroughs in medicine and genetic engineering portend a frightful horizon. Then who will let you concentrate on yourself and remember your Lord and your meeting with Him? Who will spare you a moment to switch off the earthly screen and lock the comparative window, so that you can go out into the open space of God's Custom, viewing the future with confidence and learning from history?

The kernel of history is God's sending of the Prophets (blessing and peace be upon them) for the guidance of creatures. There was a previous history in which God sent Noah, Abraham, Moses, Jesus and Muhammad (blessing and peace be upon them). There will be a future history in which we will be like cattle, if we are not imbued with the core of the Message, which made that fellow who went out from the mosque declare with forceful eloquence in the court of Rustam: "God has sent us to bring out whomever He will from the worship of human divinities to the worship of God, from the hardship of this world to its welfare, and from the injustice of the religions to the justice of Islam. He has sent us to His creatures in order to invite them to Him."

The Qur'anic Key

By the Qur'an God opened locked hearts and minds that were in their *jâhilîya* life, far from Guidance. God's Messenger (God bless him and give him peace) relieved the blessed generation that lived under his wing of their burden and the chains that were upon them.

Likewise by the Qur'an, God will produce the second Muslim creation as He produced the first one. Likewise by the Method of the Messenger (God bless him and give him peace), He will relieve us, and every generation that is guided by Revelation and Prophecy, of the stockpiles of mentalities, habits and egoisms that cloud our souls and minds and veil them from the light of Revelation.

By the Qur'an and the Prophetic Guidance, God (Exalted is He) has opened wide horizons. He has cast upon the mind that has embraced Islam, believed and practiced true devotion, suggestions for contemplation, traveling around the world, and drawing lessons from the history of past peoples. By His miraculous explanation, He has taught that mind how to express the subtlest emotions of its soul and the most refined of its intellectual movements.

The emotions of the observant soul, and the movements of the Muslim mind that is enlightened by Revelation, do not revolve around the question "how?" but rather receive the answer to the question "why?"

In directing the Muslim mind toward "how?" the Noble Qur'an wants it to reflect on what lies behind the appearance, not to be diverted by its lure.

What, do they not consider how the camel was created? (Q. 88:17)

The Qur'an urges you to ask the creature about its origin, its significance, its Creator and Shaper, instead of being interested only in the description of its form, its structure, its height and its breadth, its nourishment and its usefulness.

What has clouded the mind heedless of God in an age crammed with the descriptive "how" is our negligence of the reflective "how." That is due to the stockpiles of knowledge, the shabbiness of faith and the blindness of the hearts.

The clever minds that are skilled in posing the descriptive and functional "how" do not feel the need to pose the question "why?" The ful minds that are clever in giving an answer that is detailed, refined and substantiated by the tools of Physics, the interactions of Chemistry, the rays of diagnosis, the history of epochs, and empirical investigation, are heedless of the Hereafter and do not inquire about their Lord and Creator.

How can the shabbiness of faith and the clouding of the mind be cleared? How can faith be renewed? How can faith be revived and the mind reawakened? How can skeptical philosophical fogginess be removed from our eyes? How can the skill of the mind in posing the questions of the scientific, investigating, experimental "how" be consistent with its contemplation, awareness and recollection of the meaning of existence, the Creator of the universe, Who will raise the dead to a Day when eyes will be lowered in humility?

That is what the Qur'an opens up and the pedagogical Prophetic Method relieves for the overwhelmed mind and the chained soul. The opening brought by the Qur'an and built upon by Prophecy includes encouraging the mind to read, write and record. Muslims did not find any difficulty in studying the heritage of other peoples in terms of adoption, rejection or criticism. They had the filter of faith and the criterion of truth and falsehood. Apart from what is related to God as a Lord, Creator and Master, and directing the mind from the superficial "how" to reflection and meaning, everything else for them is futile.

The first Muslims did not recoil from seeking proof and exercising judgment. They did not neglect any of the functions of the descriptive, informative, empirical mind. On the contrary, they used them to confirm their faith that was established by the evidence of Revelation. The evidence of the scientific mind served to substantiate the testimony of faith.

The Qur'anic opening and the Prophetic Guidance enabled the Muslim mind to take long strides. During four centuries, the Muslim mind led the sciences side by side with the guidance of Science. Then the Muslim mind plunged into lethargy, until Europe's Renaissance and colonization reawakened it.

On every front, aggressive colonialism severed the links between the Muslims' past and future. It transferred them from one era to another, and exposed the lack of homogeneity and the backwardness of their scientific and empirical mind. As a consequence, the Muslims supposed that such backwardness might have a cause for which the comparative mind could find an answer. They raised the question: "Why have Muslims fallen behind while others have advanced?"

The worldly comparison has prevailed ever since. Discussion of truth and falsehood, of belief and unbelief, has been eclipsed by the turmoil of the political struggle and the historical analysis.

The westernized modernist accuses the Muslim mind of being unhistorical, whenever the latter presents an argument in support of its faith and adheres to its Qur'an. The westernized intellectual proposes modernity without faith and history without Revelation. Filled with self-confidence, arrogance and stubbornness, the Western mind arrived with colonization in the parade of its victorious weapons. Then it settled in the Muslim rising generation that was exposed to its radiation with no immunity system.

The Liberation of the Muslim Mind

Now—praise be to God!—the wakeful and active members of the Islamic uprising generation are reading the Qur'an of their Lord and studying the Method of their Prophet. The liberation of the Muslim mind represents for them a priority ahead of all priorities.

The liberation of the Muslim mind is liberation from the deeply rooted traces of the invasion that are heaped on our traditional weakness, and embodied in a westernized elite that rules and imposes its will by force, but is ultimately incapable of fulfilling its historical task and is meeting failure in every sphere.

Liberation is absolutely essential. It will enable us to recognize that our backwardness in the sciences, the branches of industry, strength and the necessities of life, is the result of our negligence of Islam and our abandonment of the Qur'an, not the opposite.

The liberation of the Muslim mind is essential, so that Muslims may have a modern economy that is competitive in the marketplace. It is essential for the establishment on firm foundations of a regional state that is prepared to gain strength through uniting with the other rising Islamic regional states. There is no stability without Islam and no Islam without unity.

There is no stability without *shûrâ,* and no unity on the basis of nationalistic democracies that are at variance with Islam, and at variance with the course of the material civilization whose peoples are joining together, leaving us to follow the mirage of the nation state that the colonizing snake has worn since the nineteenth century, and is now attempting to slough off so that we may wear it as tattered rags.

The liberation of the Muslim mind is essential, so that the Muslims may be liberated from the narrow, ethnic and regional nationalism. It is essential in order to eradicate illiteracy through the teaching of the Qur'an and the propagation of sciences. It is essential for the establishment of scientific research and the acquisition of inventive industrial skills.

The westernized thinker would say: "Let us therefore integrate into the modern age, so as to shorten the path!"

We shall reply: "Let us rather build on our own foundations, because the path of integration is closed and blocked, and the integration of Islam into unbelief is a form of apostasy. Such a path is open to frustra-

90

tion in this world and Hell in the Hereafter. Our path is independence, so that we can meet the challenges of the modern age."

The modern age is in crisis. Let us not be deluded by what others have built, such as scientific skyscrapers strewn all around and unrelated to any human project. For them, the human being has no meaning except the egoism of the strong, the wasteful consumption of the wealthy, the pleasure of the rich and the death of the poor in the Somalia of starvation and civil war, or in the Bosnia of annihilation, savage slaughter and ethnic cleansing.

The Muslims are closely linked to the world as human beings and as committed missionaries. We are the envoys of mercy, truth and justice for the world.

It is essential for the Muslim mind to be liberated from the illusion inspired in the Westernized mind, just as the devils inspire in their associates the notion that we shall not be fortunate, unless we connect our national wagon to the locomotive of the victorious civilization.

The choice of the free Muslim mind is that we should strive with all our efforts, so that, some day in the future if God will, we may lead the human caravan, while being fully aware of the content of our Message and duties toward human beings and all other creatures.

The free Muslim mind looks toward God's future destiny and toward God's requirement that we do our utmost, using strategy and tactics in the long run.

Unity is our horizon. There is no place in the world, today and tomorrow, for flimsy entities, nor any mission for ethnic groups confined in small geographic territories.

That distant horizon is near, if God will. We glimpse it from behind pressing tasks and from underneath internal and external cultural and political stockpiles.

Victory comes only from God. Glory be to God and Praise be to God. There is no god but God. God is Supremely Great. There is no might nor any power except with God, the All-High, the Almighty.

May God bless our Messenger Muhammad, the Seal of the Prophets and the Chief of the Messengers.

Our final assertion is that praise belongs to God, the Lord of All the Worlds.

Notes

1. Published by Justice and Spirituality Publishing, Iowa City, Iowa, USA, 2001.

2. In his book *Winning the Modern World for Islam* (p. 103), Imam Yassine says:

   > The word *jâhilîya* conveys a standard of judgment between *islam* and what is contrary to it. Found four times in the Qur'an, *jâhilîya* resounds with disbelief, malgovernance, the abasing of women, and the virulent fury of pagan tribalism.
   >
   > Every era has its own *jâhilîya*, its own form of tribalism, disbelief, malgovernance, profligacy, and injustice. Going to the word's root, I translate as Ignorance and Violence I capitalize so as to draw attention to these salient and permanent aspect of *jâhilîya*.
   >
   > *Jâhilîya* exists wherever humankind is ignorant of the purpose of its existence, wherever societies (whether nominally Muslim or no) are ill-governed, where woman is treated vilely, where violent instinctual passions win out in disputes, not the spirit of fairness.

3. In this Introduction, Imam Yassine uses the masculine plural forms *mu'minîn* and *muslimîn*, and the feminine plural forms *mu'minât* and *muslimât*. Since these forms are peculiar to the Arabic language, the translator has opted for the English expression "men and women who truly believe, and who surrender to the Will of Almighty God." In the sentence beginning: "True Believers, men and women . . . ," the Arabic text refers to the *mu'minîn* and the *mu'minât*.

   In the chapter Stations and a Race, Imam Yassine states that the true religion has three degrees: surrender [*islam*], faith [*îmân*] and good work [*ihsân*]. Someone who surrenders to God's Will is therefore called a *muslim*, a true believer is called a *mu'min*, and one who performs good work is called a *muhsin*. The *mu'minîn* and the *mu'minât*, being in the middle degree, are the ones addressed by God in the Qur'an to execute His Commandments. In no fewer than eighty-nine verses of the Qur'an, He addresses them with: "O you who truly believe! [*Yâ ayyuha 'lladhîna âmanû*]."

   In *Winning the Modern World for Islam* (pp. 111–112), Imam Yassine explains this concept more elaborately:

   > *Islam* is an ascent, it is not a stationary state. The first rung is that of the practicing Muslim, attentive to fulfilling the obligations the Law prescribes for every Muslim. The second rung is that of *îmân*, a higher degree, where worship and moral rectitude are on a par. The third degree, *ihsân*, is the springboard for the great spiritual journey and its infinite space. A spiritual

guide is needed for the highest degree, since the path is long and the way is full of snares. A spiritual guide, a tutor, is required until the plant of the spiritual being takes root and grows in strength.

I have spoken of rungs and degrees; I ought to have spoken of bricks and floors, since the image of a building that is being built slowly but surely is more apt. You cannot build on a void and with nothing: the progress on *islam*'s path to moral and spiritual perfection is a construction, and the fulfilling of the obligations of the Law are the bricks and cement, with prayer foremost.

4. Throughout this work, the Arabic term *ghayb* is translated as "the Unseen realm" or simply "the Unseen."

5. *Fitra* means character, natural or innate disposition, instinct, nature. In *Winning the Modern World for Islam* (p. 90), Imam Yassine explains: "*Fitra* is a Qur'anic word that denotes the psychological core of the human being. This core, this profound sense of identity and deep innate nature, is the place where faith and trust in God repose."

6. The verb *fakkara* means "to consider, to ponder over, to meditate upon."

7. The important Islamic term *shûrâ* occurs in the Qur'an:

Those who answer the call of their Lord and establish regular prayer, and who conduct their affairs by mutual Consultation [*shûrâ*] . . . (Q. 42:38).

In his Translator's Foreword to *Winning the Modern World for Islam*, Martin Jenni refers to *shûrâ* as "the Qur'anic principle of consultative self-government."

If only the nominally Muslim nations would apply that principle today, as an example of the special benefits that Islam has to offer to human society!

8. "Baptism" here represents the Arabic term *sibgha,* the root-meaning of which implies a dye or color. In a footnote to his translation of Q. 2:138, Yusuf Ali explains: "Apparently the Arab Christians mixed a dye or color in the baptismal water, signifying that the baptized person got a new color in life. We [Muslims] do not believe that it is necessary to be baptized to be saved. Our higher baptism is the 'Baptism' of God, by which we take on a color (symbolically) of God, and absorb His goodness in us."

9. The *sunna* is the exemplary practice of the Prophet (God bless him and give him peace).

10. The *umma* is the Islamic community, comprising all Muslim countries regardless of colonization-imposed geographical borders.

11. *Shâm* is the geographical area covering present-day Palestine, Lebanon, and Syria

12. Biography of the Prophet (God bless him and give him peace).

13. The basic meaning of *jihâd* is "strenuous effort." The believers are told in the Qur'an: "And strive for the sake of God with all the *jihâd* He deserves" (Q. 22:78).

> When the term is used in the sense of "holy war," its meaning is all too frequently misunderstood, especially but not only by non-Muslims. Sometimes, alas, it is willfully misrepresented—by polemicists hostile to Islam, as well as by misguided zealots within the Islamic community itself.
>
> It is certainly correct to apply the term *jihâd* to the sacred struggle against hostile unbelievers. It is a grave mistake, however, to ignore the saying of the Prophet (God bless him and give him peace) when he returned from the military expedition of Tabuk: "We have come home from the lesser *jihâd* to fight the greater *jihâd*."
>
> "The greater *jihâd*" may be understood to mean "the struggle with the devil, the ego and passionate desire." That struggle is greater, it has been said, "because of its constant duration, the extent of the exertion it demands, and the danger it entails." It may also signify "the *jihâd* of construction," with reference to "all efforts exerted in order for the Appeal of God to reach the human being, both as an individual and as a member of a society."

14. The *isrâ* is the Prophet's miraculous Night Journey to al-Aqsa Mosque in Jerusalem [al-Quds].

15. The *mi'râj* is the Prophet's Heavenly Ascension to meet God Almighty.

16. The Companions known as the *ansâr* [Helpers] were those inhabitants of Yathrib (later called Medina) who hosted and supported the Prophet (God bless him and give him peace) and the Emigrants [*muhâjirîn*] (their Meccan brothers in Islam), after the *hijra* (Exodus) to Medina.

17. Since the Jews and Christians had received the Scripture, they are referred to in the Qur'an as "the People of the Book."

18. Reported by Imam Ahmad, Abu Dawud, and an-Nasa'i.

19. *Minhâj* is the term used in the Qur'an (5:48) in the sense of method. Among the features of the Prophetic Method is authenticity, in the sense that all concepts by which it is represented are derived from either the Qur'an or the *sunna*. Such careful choice of words is not performed for the sake of difference as such, but in order to distinguish the Prophetic Method from the other worldly methods in terms of the source, the intention and the purpose.

20. "Instruction or teaching" [*ta'lîm*] is used in this book to refer to the kind of teaching that is dispensed to the Muslim mind, while "purification" [*tazkiya*] means the kind of teaching that is directed to the Muslim heart. "Education" [*tarbiya*] combines both of them.

21. Reported by Muslim and at-Tirmidhi.

22. By *hijâb* is meant not only the square of fabric worn on the woman's head, but also the decent clothing of her whole body, except what is permitted by the Law to be uncovered—her face and her hands.

23. The first member of the powerful Borgia family took the name Calixtus III (reigned 1455–1458). Pope Alexander VI (r. 1492–1503), born Rodrigo Borgia, was the father of Cesare and Lucrezia Borgia. Certain members of the family made its name notorious.

24. The *qibla* is the direction of prayer for Muslims.

25. Such commandments are derived from the Qur'an. See Q. 6:151, 152 for comparison.

26. The word *ihsân* is used here with its three meanings and dimensions:

    The highest spiritual station of Islam
    The virtue of doing good and being kind to parents and relatives
    The virtue of doing one's assigned duties with perfection and conscientiousness

27. Reported by the two Imams Ahmad and Abu Dawud and others.

28. The Goals.

29. The Prophet's Tradition.

30. The author uses the term *al-'ulûm al-kawnîya* (lit. "the cosmic sciences").

31. Methods of Research according to *Muslim Thinkers* (4th ed., p. 240).

32. Andalusia is now the southwestern region of Spain. During the time of Muslim rule, however, the whole Iberian Peninsula was referred to as Andalusia (al-Andalus in Arabic).

33. Imam Yassine quotes this statement from the above-mentioned book of Dr. Ali an-Nashshar (may God bestow His mercy upon him), who attributes it to the English author of a book concerning the genesis of humanity. Like the subsequent statements attributed to that author, this quotation is here translated from the Arabic, since the original English text is not available to the translator.

34. Tunisia today.

35. Independent judgment exercised by Muslim jurists in the absence of unambiguous rulings in the Qur'an or the *sunna*.

36. This was said at the time of the Soviet invasion of Afghanistan.

37. A distinguished Algerian Muslim thinker of the 20th century.

38. Comprehensive and sincere advice.

By the Same Author

IN ENGLISH:
Winning the Modern World for Islam, 2000
Memorandum: To Whom It May Concern, 2000

IN FRENCH:
La Révolution à l'heure de l'islam, 1980
Pour un dialogue avec l'élite occidentalisée, 1980
Islamiser la modernité, 1998
Mémorandum: à qui de droit, 2000

IN GERMAN:
Memorandum: An den Berechtigten, 2000

IN SPANISH:
Memorandùm: a quien correspond, 2000

IN ARABIC:
Islam between the Appeal and the State, 1971
Tomorrow *Islam!* 1972
Islam—or the Flood: An Open Letter to the King of Morocco, 1974
The Prophetic Method, 1982 (4 editions)
Islam and the Challenge of Marxism-Leninism, 1987 (2 editions)
Exemplary Men, 1989 (1st in the series *Al-Ihssân*)
Introductions to the Method, 1989 (2 editions)
Islam and the Challenge of Secular Nationalism, 1989 (2 editions)
Reflections on Islamic Jurisprudence and History, 1990 (3 editions)
Spiritual Gems (A Collection of Poems) 1992
The Muslim Mind on Trial, 1994 (2 editions)
A Dialog with Honorable Democrats, 1994
Letter of Reminder, 1995 (1st in the series *Rassa'il Al-Ihssân*)
On the Economy, 1995

By the Same Author

Letter to Students and to all Muslims, 1995 (2nd in the series *Rassa'il Al-Ihssân*) (2 editions)

Guide to Believing Women (in 2 volumes), 1996 (2 editions)

Shûra and Democracy, 1996

Poetic Exhortations, 1996 (3rd in the series *Rassa'il Al-Ihssân*)

Dialog of the Past and the Future, 1997

Dialog with an Amazighit Friend, 1997

Spirituality [*Al-Ihssân*] (1st volume), 1998

Spirituality [*Al-Ihssân*] (2nd volume), 1999

Memorandum: To Whom It May Concern, 2000

Winning the Modern World for Islam, 2000

Bunches of Grapes (A Collection of Poems, 1st volume) 2000

Justice: Islamists and Power, 2000

The Scholastic Treatise, 2000

Caliphate and Monarchy, 2000

N.B. All of these works have been published in closed circulation, since the author (and his thoughts) as well as the Justice and Spirituality association *al-'Adl wal-Ihsân* are subjected to strict surveillance.